Called to Healing

Called to Healing

Reflections
on the Power of Earth's Stories
in Women's Lives

Jean Troy-Smith

State University of New York Press

Published by
State University of New York Press, Albany

For information, address State University of New York Press,
State University Plaza, Albany, N.Y., 12246

Production by Diane Ganeles
Marketing by Theresa Abad Swierzowski

Library of Congress Cataloging-in-Publication Data

Troy-Smith, Jean.
    Called to healing : reflections on the power of Earth's stories in
women's lives / Jean Troy-Smith.
        p.   cm.
    Includes bibliographical references and index.
    ISBN 0–7914–2975–X (alk. paper). — ISBN 0–7914–2976–8 (pbk. :
alk. paper)
    1. Spiritual life.   2. Human ecology in literature.   3. Nature in
literature.   4. Women and literature.   5. Feminist criticism.
    6. Spiritual healing.   7. Storytelling.   8. Sacred space.   9. Myth
I. Title.
    BL304.T76   1993
    398'.082—dc20   95–33614
                                                                  CIP

10 9 8 7 6 5 4 3 2 1

To Mom and Dad
Dale William Troy: September 24, 1902—January 5, 1983
Ethel Knobbe Troy: November 24, 1916—September 12, 1994

Peace, at last

Contents

Foreword   ix

Acknowledgments   xiii

Part I: The Stories Begin   1

Part II: Storytelling and Truthtelling:
"I remember and I recall"   17

Part III: "Tell me a story that's true"   57
    Dulcie Adelaid: a woman from the Earth in
    Cactus Thorn by Mary Austin   65

    The Journeys of Gertie and Mrs. Anderson
    in *The Dollmaker* by Harriette Arnow   89
    Gertie in Kentucky   89
    Gertie in Detroit   98
    Mrs. Anderson: portrait of an angel   109

    Revisioning goddess consciousness
    in *The Fires of Bride* by Ellen Galford   117

    A weave of women in *Send My Roots Rain*
    by Ibis Gómez-Vega   143

Part IV: Sacred Spaces:
    the need to name and claim them in our lives   171

Contents

Notes   183

Works Cited   197

Index   203

Foreword

In this thoughtful book, Jean Troy-Smith blends the fictional and the factual to illustrate the literary power of personal narrative by focusing on specific themes that link both the teller and the listener/reader in ways that allow each to construct a meaningful sense of self. As an act of *experiencing an experience, Called to Healing* beckons readers to reposition themselves against the familiar in order to acknowledge new readings of well-known literature. From such reading/experiencing, readers may find themselves connecting with and giving voice to their own emotional experiences that connect with the literature/stories in this book— a first step in reclaiming and writing their own lives.

As a reflection on EARTH stories in women's lives, this text may be read in the tradition of Native American Storytelling; that is, each part seems to concern itself with different levels of mythological time, in this case women's time, appropriate for different ritual occasions marking a journey. Part One on remembering may suggest the tribal relation of story to the creation of gods-goddesses and the world. This section challenges us to remember what for some may be "dangerous memories." Memories may emerge as stories that represent "political theories" of positionality as the writings of Hannah Arendt have suggested. From principled understanding more than fact, memories represented in stories may stand as a response/analysis to domination.

ix

To continue in Native American tradition, Part Two might be read as a narrative differentiating gods/goddesses. For example, "the grandmother image" in Paula Gunn Allen's *Spider Woman's Granddaughters* is taken from Grandmother Spider in Native creation myth. Here Gunn Allen likens weaving to storytelling suggesting the merging of roles and cultures. The traditional housebuilder suggested by the female spider in Gunn Allen's rendering, through a creative act is both political and poetic, weaves a new web of meaning when readers imagine/reconceptionalize existing social structures that can map onto a cultural zone. The literature Troy-Smith calls upon in this section to illustrate the transformative power of EARTH stories also weaves a new web of meaning.

Part Three may be read as a continuation of the project of mapping new cultural spaces as EARTH stories suggest ways perhaps women especially may make whole their often fragmented lives—a fragmentation that in no small measure occurs from not knowing how to respond to domination. In Native American tradition, healing responses come from connections to the earth. The third part of the Native ritual journey is, therefore, suggested in the theme *Sacred Spaces* where connections are named and claimed. Claiming these spaces signals the voicing of women's oral (tribal) histories, the third level of mythological time in which tribal histories are formed. Identifying with sacred spaces, narrating their import in healing suggests a *gift of power*—not power over but power with.

Troy-Smith connects with and claims EARTH's sacred spaces as does Terry Tempest Williams in *Refuge* and Florence Krall in *Ecotone*. She vulnerably makes her journey/struggle apparent as both Tempest Williams and Krall do. By working in the overlap between textual spaces and cultural spaces, by introducing social changes while maintaining traditions, Troy-Smith, like Krall and Tempest Williams, creates a story we must take seriously. For if the literary power of narrative has the potential to connect the experiences of author/teller and reader/listener, then we should all sit back and experience the experience. As Linda Boynton wrote recently in a course on narrative:

> Because narrative joins the experiences of author and reader making new soil, the seeds that begin to grow create a hybrid of new ideas that enlarge the universe for the reader and everyone he/she comes into contact with. As the reader grabs a handful of this loam and sifts it down to seeds and stones, the stones, those new perceptions that appear in direct opposition to the precepts that have so far governed how we live, are now in the open. At least for awhile, if we choose to bury them again, we live with the consequences. But the landscape will never quite be the same.

In the tradition, then, of Leslie Marmon Silko's *Storyteller*, Jean Troy-Smith seeks to initiate the reader into a new perception of worldmaking through story. Indeed, it is a perception that may change both the reader and her or his world. By using different modes of storytelling from fiction to personal narrative, Troy-Smith stimulates women's oral tradition on paper and creates as Maxine Green suggests a *landscape for learning*.

Diane DuBose Brunner

Acknowledgments

I did not make this journey alone; indeed I could not. Many other people—and their stories—walked my path with me. In an earlier version, this book was my dissertation for my Ph.D. in Literature from The Union Institute in Cincinnati, Ohio. Because of Union's unique approach to graduate work, I was able to write theory from my personal history.

My committee, collectively and individually, were some of my guides: my core advisor, Martha Crunkleton, who, as she listened to me go through many moments of darkness, guided me into as many moments of light. She heard through my questions and anxieties and enabled me to understand what were the philosophic foundations that shored up not only my Ph.D. work, but my life's work. Elizabeth Minnich, who, in evaluating my work as the outside reader, created a perspective of which I had not been aware; it was Elizabeth who showed me that I was crossing interdisciplinary fields for which there as yet were no names. *And* she encouraged me to continue. Karen Elias and Geri De Luca, my adjunct experts, at times took me by the literary hand to lead me through some fairly tangled passages; they are both such clear writers in their own right. Joan Spencer and Margaret Blanchard were my committee peers who gave me more than what their duty on my committee commissioned them to do; their positive and sustaining encouragement forced me deeper into myself than I wanted to go.

Then there is Fr. Julian von Duerbeck, O.S.B., a former student of mine, now a Benedictine monk and expert on world religions. In May, 1990, he was visiting our family, heard my story, and then supplied me with a long list of books on goddess spirituality; he also recounted his experience of having lunch with Luisah Teisch.

Nancy Osborne, librarian and friend, combined the two roles during my research and writing time; books and articles appeared via campus mail on a regular basis with the notation, "Jean, Nancy."

My husband, John, did not teach the summer of 1992 so that I was free to write. He was not only father and mother to our two sons, he was what Tillie Olsen calls "the essential angel of the house." He also found me an apartment in Oswego, N.Y., as a hideaway for that summer so that I was truly free to write.

The ink was hardly dry on my diploma when another colleague and friend, Virginia Fichera, urged me to get my manuscript published, refusing to let me become disheartened with rejections.

My brother, Ron Troy, is in the health-care field. After I graduated, he acted as a personal agent. He sent copies of my manuscript to health-care friends. I knew there was something worthwhile in my manuscript when one of the physicians wrote him that I should try to publish part of the manuscript in a journal that accepted articles on success stories of survivors of post-traumatic-stress syndrome! I had crossed the boundary of the usually separate disciplines of health and literature.

At SUNY Press, Lois Patton had the fortitude to not only accept my work but to be excited about it. No matter what turn our conversations take, each time we talk I glean something from her to make this book better.

Lorraine Anderson for our ongoing conversation about women and nature via letters, notes, and e-mail; I responded to her book with a long, impassioned letter, and we have kept in touch ever since. Ibis Gómez-Vega, meeting through her novel and continuing with a "pen-pal" friendship.

My newest journey-walker is Diane Brunner, who took on the task of writing a foreword that placed my work in the context of this new field that as yet has no precise, definable name; no name, but it does have a tradition that is as old as the time when women and men first walked this home called Earth.

And there are my two children, Jason and Owen. Without them, I would not have made this journey.

These guides, showing up when needed, verify my belief that is the unifying thread of this text: when we find ourselves fragmented from life's experiences, it is Earth who calls us to healing in Her power to tell us stories; we just need to be open to hear them.

Part I

The Stories Begin

Called To Healing was born from a basic human need to story personal experience. Humans have this need to story, but all of us do not organize our experiences into written form. Usually a focal event precipitates that organizing. For me, the event was a violent incident that involved one of my children. It was an event that caused me profound grieving, grieving that, in retrospect, was necessary in order for me to see that I had been living most of my life uprooted from my Self. It was an incident that gave me the impetus to find that Self. In March of 1990 Owen was deliberately shot in the eye by a neighbor boy with a BB gun. In the end, my son did not lose his eye; he did not even lose any vision, a circumstance we were not to know for about twenty-four hours as we waited for surgery results. That act and its aftermath, however, marked the beginning of a journey for me that would end with the writing of this book.

The event had begun as I left our house to pick up my older son, Jason, at his friend's house. It was five in the afternoon. Owen (I thought) was outside playing with friends. Jason called for me to come and pick him up. I told him that I would, as soon as I could find Owen so that he could come with me. He was nine years old; I had never left him home alone. As I left the house to find Owen, I met a force outside of my door that was so strong, it pushed me backwards. I looked around. There was no wind. The air, in fact, was still. There was no one there. Nothing was under my feet that could have tripped me up. Instinctively I thought: "Something has happened to Owen." I ran from the door and down the porch to find him. He wasn't out front or down the street. I rationalized that he had gone next door to play with the two boys who lived there. Again I felt how still the air was, as before a storm. Living in Oswego for all these years has accustomed me to near-constant air movement, calm and noisy, caressing and ferocious because the city is situated on the southern shore of Lake Ontario. I stood on the sidewalk for a moment, then shook my head to dismiss the message: *something has happened to Owen.* I came back to our house, got in the car and drove to pick up Jason. I was gone twelve minutes. When I pulled into our driveway with Jason, my neighbor met me at the car. "Jean, Owen's been hurt. He's at the hospital."

"Was he hit by a car?" I asked.

"No," she replied. My mind started racing, trying to think of other possibilities.

"What happened?" I asked.

"He's been shot," she said.

I collapsed behind the steering wheel like a puppet whose strings the maker had abandoned. "Shot?" I said. "Is he dead?"

"No. He was shot in the eye."

"Who did it?"

"Timmy. John is with him."

In the twelve minutes I was gone, three things had happened: my husband had come home; five neighborhood boys who had witnessed the shooting had walked Owen home from around the corner and down the next street where the incident happened; and Owen and John had gone to the hospital, four blocks from our house.

As I heard the words, *he's been shot,* I knew that not only had Earth's non-verbal "voice" called to me as the force that had pushed me backwards as I walked out the door, but I had ignored that voice, as I had been ignoring similar messages from Earth and Self for decades. It was that insight that also caused me to momentarily collapse behind the wheel of the car that fateful day. Finally, I acknowledged the voice, and this time would choose not to ignore it.

Two more such incidents happened shortly afterwards that called to me to begin my journey to Self. Anytime there is a hospitalization, however brief, that involves a gun, the hospital personnel are required to call the police to file a report. When a police officer took Owen's statement about the incident, one of the questions he was asked was, "Where was your mother?"

"She had gone to get my brother."

"Then your mother was not at home?"

"No. My mother was not at home."

Until that day, I had never left Owen alone for one minute, let alone twelve of them. And now, written in the police report was, *my mother was not at home.* That I had gone to pick up my other son was not entered into the report. I asked, "why not?" The officer replied that that part was not pertinent to the case. Both John and I were with Owen when he gave his statement, but, "Where was your father?" was never asked. That the report only noted the presence or absence of the mother from the home still causes some anger in me: not only had I followed the cultural rules for being "the good mother" for all the minutes I had been a mother, except those critical twelve, the choice to leave Owen and pick up Jason had been a "Sophie's choice." I was forced to choose an "either-or."

It may have taken me decades to finally heed Earth's call to healing, but once I did listen and then chose to continue listening, I acted on what I heard. In May, I "heard" about The Union Institute and its unique approach to doctoral studies, wrote for materials and participated in the entry colloquium in October. My journey/story had begun.

The Union Institute approaches doctoral studies through a learner-centered, non-traditional way. I took advantage of that way and incorporated into my research not only the culture and history of women back to pre-biblical times but also the culture and history of my uprooted moorings. I came to understand that the Self listens and learns differently from the way the self listens and learns. I came to understand that what the Self hears is Earth's voice, heard through Earth's stories. This was the voice that called me to heal the wounds from decades of inner uprootedness.

As I realized this insight and began to put my story on paper, I knew that I would need to use some words differently to describe what I was learning. Therefore, I have made some distinctions between identical words that carry different meanings. When I refer to *self* with a lower-case *s*, I mean the mundane, ordinary, routinely-patterned, day-to-day self that operates as part of society. When I use *Self* with an upper-case *S*, I mean the core that is each unique individual. When I use *earth* with a lower-case *e*, I refer to the dirt that is the ground on which we walk. When I use *Earth* with an upper-case *E*, I mean the planet that, in our vast universe, is our home.

Here is my story of how I wrestled with taking a path in life that I had no intention of ever taking, never knew that it was possible *to* take, but once I saw that it was there to take, knew that if I did not, the wound created by that act on my son would never heal in me. I had a strong enough will to know that I did not want to go through the rest of my life with the sense of the uprooted and fragmented self that began to dominate my life. So even at the points in my journey where quitting the search would have been both easy and socially acceptable, I chose to push through the fear that can accompany one into the unknown.

In my search/journey to connect self to Self, I read and listened to stories from women (and a few men) who have made similar journeys and came through those journeys having experienced new discoveries. For me, I knew that the path to wholeness would be found in stories, because stories in and of themselves hold healing properties; it is one of their attributes.

It is in this personal appreciation for story, then, that I turned to the work that became the healing experience for me. Through this journey and the stories I heard and read, I have another way of evaluating and living life. I have not made radical changes in the external manifestations of who I am. Inwardly, however, self is rooting to Self and I, like the seed that sends roots down into the soil while simultaneously sending shoots up toward the sun, I am growing wholly. *That* is the result of the choice I made in March of 1990 when Earth called me, as it called me many times in the past but I chose not to hear; however, this time I chose to listen and to act.

One story that I was drawn to early on in this journey to Self is "Magic in a World of Magic" by Anne Cameron. In it, the young narrator tells a story concerning two important life-questions that I asked myself after my world was turned upside down that day in March 1990: "Who am I?" and "How did I come to be?" This young narrator is invited to join a circle of older women telling stories; one of the older women is her grandmother. She is eager to please her grandmother, so she brought her grandmother gifts: "I brought juice for her throat and food for her belly . . . but what did I bring for her spirit, [Granny asked]. A person can go days without water, weeks without food, but only hours without hope or love. And what did I have for her soul?" For Granny, what nourishes her soul is a story. When the girl says she is not certain what to tell about, the grandmother charges her with: "Tell me how you came to be and who you are." In telling her story, the narrator goes back to, "Long ago and far away . . . , long before there were Authorities, there were people. . . . And these people lived in families, with the oldest mother as their wise one, and everything belonged to the women, and all women were mother to all children."[1]

Vickie L. Sears writes a story called "Sticktalk" in which her narrator learns from a Medicine Stick who she is and how she came to be. Medicine Stick tells the woman who found her: "I am a root once ground-grown and anchored into the earth. As are you.

Always." The Stick reminds her: "I am also a water floater. . . . And, I am a maker of fire." In other words, this root, of and from the Earth, represents the element of earth, lives complementary to water and is known to give her life to fire and be transformed, as is she who is the listener of Stick's story. "Listen in yourself to the old parts. They are still good" says Stick. Each day since finding Stick, the narrator touches her "in leaving or coming," and she thanks the "Hall of Grandmothers and the Creator" for placing Stick in her path. This listener in the story who finds Stick lying on the ground is in need of a story to nourish her spirit. She is in a phase of her life where she feels eternally lonely and disconnected from life, uprooted. Knowing that her soul needs to be fed, Stick nourishes her with the story of "how she came to be and who she is."[2]

Another question I found myself asking as I read and listened to stories is "what truths are they telling me?" *They* refers to the stories, the story tellers, and the characters in the stories. To find answers to this question, I took the words *story* and *truth*, placed them on a metaphorical turnstile so that I could look at the different facets of these words in order to see, in the turning, what the facets told me about the *they*.

The stories I have listened to and read that make sense to me on this journey have their roots in ancient times. They are stories whose roots go deep into goddess consciousness, course through thousands of years of our planet's historical veins, and send up shoots in today's writings about nature. They begin with sentences like: "When the world was new and young"; "'Did Mama sing every day?'"; "Nature has been for me, for as long as I can remember, a source of solace, inspiration, adventure, and delight, a home, a teacher, a companion"; "Preserved in a cave sanctuary for over twenty thousand years, a female figure speaks to us about the minds of our early Western ancestors"; "I was born in the city of the Voudoun—New Orleans, Louisiana"; "Long before there was an earth and long before there were people called human, there was a Sky World"; "Together with a few human beings, dead and living, and their achievements, trees are what I most love and revere"; "I belong to a Clan of one-Breasted Women."

They are the stories of Demeter, Sarah, Lorraine, Inanna, Luisah, Beth, Hildegarde, and Terry. There is something in these stories that I hear, and I say, "I know that story; that is my story, too." They are stories that tell me that being born female did not condemn me to a belief that, therefore, I am profane, unclean, put on this Earth only to continue to release evil and pain in the world when I release new life through birth. They are stories that proclaim that the female is sacred. I present my discoveries in Part II called, "Storytelling and Truthtelling: 'I Remember and I Recall.'"

In Part III I present an eco-feminist, reader-response analysis of four fictional narratives. The narratives I have chosen are *Cactus Thorn* by Mary Austin, *The Dollmaker* by Harriette Arnow, *The Fires of Bride* by Ellen Galford and *Send My Roots Rain* by Ibis Gómez-Vega. The women who authored these narratives created women characters whose lives are formed and transformed by their relationship to Earth. At certain junctures in their lives, the women characters are uprooted from Earth and from the core of the Self. A woman so uprooted is alienated, fractured, not whole. Unless that woman finds a way to root, she cannot heal to wholeness. I look closely at the journeys of these women characters during their experience of being uprooted, and examine if and/or how they reroot themselves.

Part IV examines the complex meanings of *sacred space*. As my journey continued, I discovered that I had a need to find an inviolate place where I could feel safe to ask the questions that required me to be courageous on finding the answers; or, if I could not find the answers, at least have the opportunity to delve as deeply into the questions as I needed to delve. The everyday world became both frightening and inauthentic for me, because the questions I was asking were not the kind to be probed between folding loads of laundry and picking kids up from school. I needed space that provided me with uninterrupted time that I controlled.

The women in the stories that I was drawn to and the women who told the stories I discovered had that same need.

Thus I drew solace and instruction from their journey's lessons, and I write these reflections in Part IV. I suggest that sacred space—finding it and naming it— is necessary for uprooted women to root themselves with Earth in order to begin the process of healing their Selves and their Beings. I found the process of rooting also heals the Earth, the same Earth that helps these women to be healed and nourished on their life's journey. It was my most joyous discovery, the ongoing, interwoven relationship between Earth and Self, and that discovery—and the writing of it—that rerooted my self to Self. I gained the perspective that I had been actively seeking since that fateful day in March of 1990.

Mircea Eliade suggested a journey into the sacred in the 1950s. He argued that all nature is capable of revealing itself as a "cosmic sacralit." Acknowledging the presence of alienating, profane space, he believes that, properly speaking, "there is no longer any world, there are only fragments of a shattered universe, an amorphous mass consisting of an infinite number of more or less neutral places in which [men and women] move, and are governed and driven by the obligations of an existence incorporated into an industrial society."[3] The experience of sacred space, says Eliade, makes a meaningful life possible. I found that the manifestation of the *sacred* in space creates the center of one's Self. Thus human life can only be lived in sacred places, because it is only in those sacred places that people participate fully in their Being.

To prepare myself for this research, I sought out life stories that have nurtured and enlightened me on my own particular life's journey. "Which stories have I needed to know to move me along my journey?" I asked myself. I found that a story appealed to me if, when I intereacted with it, I saw another facet of where I came from, who I am, and how I can cope with what the world —culture— tells me is true. Often what the world tells me is true is in contradiction to what Earth tells me is true. The resonance of such an interaction taught me how I came to be, who I am and what, in effect, are my life's truths.

A woman's journey, however, has never been as visible or as valued as a man's journey. There is ample history supporting this position. In the Judeo-Christian tradition, for example, the men wrote the laws and held "the truth." These laws live on through the pages of the Bible where a religious hierarchy exists with a single male deity at the pinnacle. Women were subsumed into the generic "he" and told that "he" included "she," (but "she" did not include "he.") Even though Genesis 1:27 says that, "God created man in His image; in the divine image He created him; male and female he created them," females have been denied visibility and value. Like the Declaration of Independence that espouses, "All men are created equal," white women and people of color were excluded from the generic "men," that "men" meant men, white men, particularly white men with property.

Nicole Brossard laments this cultural invisibility and marginalization of women. She tells readers that because the dominant language users have attempted to erase the female, it is important that each woman tells her story. She says that even though "it is getting late . . . each woman must repeat her story at least once in her life, with passion and with hope, as a kind of inscription." This is an imperative for each woman because not only is "the reality of woman . . . not the reality of men" but because women have been written out of history. Each woman telling/writing her story will show the desire "to assert herself in language by actualizing with its help a manner of being . . . , a manner of seeing . . ., and a manner of thinking . . . because "where there is Masculine, one sees no *feminine*." Brossard goes on to say that to render the woman visible "is a writing task which necessitates shifts in meanings as yet unedited in the imaginary realm of language."[4]

A woman telling her own story, finding her own truth outside of her relation to the male, is not a new idea. It is as old as Inanna,

Isis, Astarte, Hathor and Sky Woman. It is as old as the tale of Mother Earth is old. In "Why Women Need the Goddess: Phenomenological, Psychological, and Political Reflections," Carol Christ acknowledges the truth of women. She writes that, "the simplest and most basic meaning of the symbol of the goddess is the acknowledgement of the legitimacy of female power as a beneficient and independent power . . . that [women] will no longer look to men or male figures as saviors." In fact, women need not look to *female* figures as saviors either, because women do not need to be saved: "the divine principle, . . . the sustaining power, is in herself."[5] Women, then, can choose to worship no male deity again. We are whole, self-sufficient, meaning-centered, and sacred.

However, women need not burn all bridges, forging individual paths with neither support from those around us nor ancestral memory of those who went before us. Rather, we can acknowledge and rejoice in the fact that certain images of the goddess and what they represent are reflections of what is in all of us as women. That image can be the Buffalo Woman of the Plains Indians; Kali, a goddess of India; the African goddess, Oshun of the ancient Yoruba tribe; or the powerful Celtic triple goddess called Bride, or Bridget. To acknowledge them is to acknowledge that it is the Earth that is life-giver, that Her treasures feed, clothe and sustain us while we live, and that when we die, she accepts us back into her.[6]

Some of the stories that I present are informed by the writings of women scholars who have personally journeyed to sacred sites of goddess centers in such diverse places as Sumer, Ireland, Greece, Hungary and India: Merlin Stone, Mary Condron, Riane Eisler, Carol Christ, Buffie Johnson, Marija Gimbutas, Elinor Gadon, Z Budapest. Some of these writers have experienced the life of a woman-centered culture, longed for by Nicole Brossard, some time in their growing-up years: Paula Gunn Allen, Luisah Teish, Carol Lee Sanchez, Anne Cameron, Alice Walker are a few who know that experience of a woman-centered culture, usually (but not always) from the culture of their family. Living that life led them to uncover the truths of their existence as women with their own histories in their respective cultures and in their respective times.

I have never been to the sites designated as goddess sites where anthropologists and historians have uncovered caves and labyrinths and passages that hold artifacts pointing to a goddess culture existing for thousands of years before the patriarchy. I have, however, participated in a culture where the female energy of my mother's mother (a midwife), and of my mother and her six sisters nurtured and centered my growing-up energy in a time of strong patriarchal dominance: World War II, the post-war period, and the Eisenhower years.

The knowing and the energy, hidden, lying dormant in me for over four decades came alive and gave me the desire to research more about my half of the species and its history when I read *The Chalice and the Blade* by Riane Eisler in 1987. My world view changed dramatically when I finished reading this book. Though there had been other books written on goddesses before Ms. Eisler's, I had found no reference to them; Ms. Eisler's book marked a crossroads for me.

In the past, when I had asked the question, "Where did I come from?", the answer I was given was "from God," with emphasis on *God* as *He*. Reading this book made me realize that the vague feeling of uprootedness that had been with me from childhood (I never quite "belonged" anywhere) came because no one had ever answered my question *Where did I come from?* in a satisfactory way. I knew that I did not come from anyone I had read about in the Bible, and until Ms. Eisler's text I did not know that there was a pre-biblical tradition of the goddess, my source of Being, the tradition from whence I came.

Learning not only *when* God was a woman but *that* God was a woman, I came to realize that if *I* had been lied to about where I came from, so had countless others. Reading Riane Eisler's book started me researching whatever I could find on the topic of pre-biblical spirituality. The more I read, the more I became aware that not only had I been lied to, but that the lie about coming from a male god precipitated other lies being told as truth: males are superior to and hold property and sexual rights over females; and males, being God's image on Earth, have dominion over all other Earth creatures, from wolves to redwoods to females. Thus males have been given a right to conquer and plunder prairies, rain forests, and the seas' fish population in the name of progress and profit and development.

Childhood memories of physical abuse started to come forth to me, and those senseless acts of being hit for no apparent reason started to make sense—if there can be sense found in senseless acts of violence. Adult males could treat women and children in any way they found suitable because of the truths held by the culture, in particular the community where I grew up. A man could hit me "for my own good," and I was to be grateful. That man could be father, uncle, even neighbor. After all, as male, he held the God-given power to discipline me so that when I grew up and married, I would know my place, be a God-fearing woman. I would have been trained "right": *right* meaning that I would grow up to be the silenced woman, as I had been reared to be the silenced girl. It was said of me: "she's such a good girl, so quiet. She obeys well." Yes, I hoped that to obey would mean that I would not be hit anymore. That was a false hope, because I was hit for more than having transgressed a rule; I was hit at random.

In my childhood, there was another interesting pecking order: men could hit women and children, but women and children could not hit men. However, women could hit children if the men gave them permission to do so. Thus the men were placed in the position of being God's judge and jury on Earth. Ironically, there was someone who had power over even the men: the local priest. He held the power to condemn any and all of us to Hell for all eternity. He told us often that he had that power—and that we were condemned. From this perspective of male superiority and dominance, physical abuse was condoned and practiced in my family, my community, and my church.

The second book that had a dramatic effect on me was one that was published in April 1991 called *Sisters of the Earth: Women's Prose and Poetry About Nature* by Lorraine Anderson. What Ms. Anderson wrote about in *Sisters of the Earth* answered a question nagging me for years, a question that I could not find any information and *collected* research on: where were the women role models to whom nature mattered as much as, but not in the same way that it mattered to the men, from whom I would know, "Who am I?" Where were the female Aldo Leopolds, the John Muirs, the Henry David Thoreaus? Indeed, where was Thoreau's *mother*? She was my metaphor. I would ask people in a rhetorical manner: "And what of Henry's mother? Did she, too, write about ants or wilderness or war and we do not have her papers? Did she write some of the works credited to her son? Was her perspective the same as or different from her son's on ants or wilderness or war?"

Yes, I had Willa Cather and Rachel Carson and, of late, Annie Dillard as role models. But I knew "deep down," from my growing-up years in farm country near Aldo Leopold's home and from participating in human interactions with the Earth, that there were more than three women who were up to the task of writing their experiences with and their appreciation of the Earth. My interactions with the Earth, namely the woods in back of our house, the fields at the bottom of our hill, and our immense garden were my sources for consolation and solace in my childhood. I had not written about those interactions but I had had them, and I remembered them.

The reason I could not find the information I sought was that it was scattered; it had never been collected until Lorraine Anderson undertook the task. Indeed there are such women. In fact, there are so many that Ms. Anderson found that she needed to limit her collection; she chose to include only women of the United States, and then she had to limit those choices.[7]

In the four fictional narratives that comprise Part III, I follow the theory put forth by Elizabeth A. Flynn in her essay "Gender and Reading," which espouses a feminist reader-response criticism. "Self and other, reader and text," she writes, "interact in such a way that the reader learns from the experience without losing critical distance; reader and text interact with a degree of mutuality. . . . Self and other remain distinct and so create a kind of dialogue."[8]

Reader-response criticism holds that the reader plays a vitally important role in shaping the literary experience. Reader-response critics, then, are ones who share the conviction that readers of texts play as important a role in interpreting those texts as the writers who wrote the texts and the narrators within the texts who tell the story. Reader-response criticism is a critical method that assesses what exists between the reader and the text, not what *ought* to be or what is *good*. Its purpose is to describe, not to evaluate.

There are clear advantages to using reader-response criticism. First of all, such a method acknowledges the active engagement of both the writer and the reader; it emphasizes the reader's comprehending a text by mediating the symbolic knowledge and experience expressed in the text with the knowledge and experience existing in the mind and the heart of the reader.

Such an interaction acknowledges the literary contributions of both text and reader and thereby provides a voice for the text and a framework for the construction of the meaning of the text. Thus, the meaning of a text depends on the interaction of the reader, the writer, and the interpretative strategies employed. What a reader gets out of a text depends on what that reader brings to the text.

Second, a reader-response criticism confronts the common ground taken up by both the experiences suggested in the text and the real experiences of the reader; between the reading *self* and the *other*: text. Reader-response criticism finds its fulfillment, Flynn argues, when the critical, receptive reader achieves a balance of detachment and involvement, when the reader integrates past experiences with the experiences created by the text. Past and present are synthesized into a new experience from which, Flynn concludes, "the reader is transformed, renewed."

If the *reader* integrates past experiences with the experiences created by the text, then the gender and philosophy of the reader are important. Flynn discovered this importance when, in the spring of 1980, she and two male colleagues team-taught a class of first-year composition with fifty-two students: twenty-six women and twenty-six men. The students were to respond to three short stories chosen by the three professors. The students' responses were the data for research in gender and reading. The results of the data provided the seed for Flynn's conclusion that the gender of the reader plays a significant role in reader-response criticism.

Patrocinio P. Schweickart, Flynn's co-editor, adds to the notion that the gender of a reader influences the critical response when she writes that the *philosophy* of a reader matters. For Schweickart, it is important to know whether or not a reader, particularly a reader of a female text, is a feminist. She claims that:

> feminist readings of female texts are motivated by the need "to connect," to recuperate, or to formulate—they come to the same thing—the context, the tradition, that would link women writers to one another, to women readers and critics, and to the larger community of women.[9]

The problem of assessing the impact of a reader's gender and philosophy on the perception of a literary text reflects what Elizabeth Minnich calls a "root problem." She writes, the problem is that:

> A few privileged men defined themselves as constituting mankind/ humankind and simultaneously saw themselves as akin to what mankind/humankind ought to be in fundamental

ways that distinguish themselves from all others. Thus, at the
same time they removed women and nonprivileged men within
their culture and other cultures from "mankind," they justified
that exclusion on the grounds that the excluded were by nature
and culture "lesser" people. . . . Their notion of who was properly
human was *both* exclusive *and* hierarchical with regard to those
they took to be properly subject to them—women in all roles;
men who worked with their hands; male servants and slaves;
women and men of many other cultures.[10]

The women writers whose works I have chosen to consider are
"lesser people," as are the characters whom they develop.

My interpretations of the fictional narratives in Part III will be
informed by my gender, my philosophy, and my life experiences. A
feminist reader-response reading of the texts, woven together with
personal experience, conversations with friends and colleagues,
and library research provides the basis for my interpretations.

This is a book, then, about several women, real and fictive, on
their journeys into both sacred and profane spaces as they remember and recall the truths that tell them how they came to be and
who they are. Some break through to discovery; some do not.
Those who do, learn that it is Earth's stories that root the self to
Self and connect them with all that lives. It is Earth that tells them
how they came to be and who they are.

Part II

Storytelling and Truthtelling: "I remember and I recall"

"What happened?" asks the mother of her child when he comes to her crying. He is three years old and was playing with a friend. He tells his story. "What happened?" we ask of poets and philosophers and scientists when we want to know how the world began. They tell us in their poetry, essays, and tracts. "What happened?" people asked Rachel Carson when the eagles were dying, their eggs cracking before the embryos could form to live life beyond the shell. She tells us the story in *Silent Spring*.

The telling of stories goes back before the dawn of recorded time. We know that because the "dawn of recorded time" begins with the writing down of the stories that had been told in the oral tradition for millennia. Merlin Stone writes that there is documentation from about the year 2400 B.C.: "literature and surviving artifacts" on "the invasion by the northern people." There is "suggestive evidence" that there were earlier invasions dating back to 4,000 B.C., "before the time of written records." What is important about these invasions is that the northern Indo-European and Indo-Aryan tribes that invaded the southern tribes of the Mediterranean area brought with them male deities and an attitude that they were a superior people based on their ability to conquer the more culturally developed, goddess-centered peoples. In their conquering over the centuries, they replaced the goddesses with a supreme male deity by severely punishing those who did not worship the male deity. One method of forcing the change was to write down their stories infused by that values and beliefs, thus usurping and, for thousands of years, suppressing any memory of goddess spirituality.[1]

Stone quotes theologian Sheila Collins who believes that "theology is ultimately political," that determining categories of what is good and what is evil, of how human communities "deify the transcendent" has more to do with " 'the power dynamics of the social systems which create the theologies than with the spontaneous revelation of truth from another quarter.' "[2] Truth told through spontaneous revelation, then, is not what will necessarily prevail. Theologies created to justify a conquering point of view are theologies *not* created from spontaneous revelations of truth. Therefore, the remembering and the recalling by the conquering tribes that forced their beliefs in male deities may be based on false constructs.

One of those false constructs is illuminated by Mary Condron in a section of her book, *The Serpent and the Goddess*, that she calls "The Myth of Objectivity." In that section she writes: "most writers assume that they are 'objective' and, therefore, can arrive at 'truth'; feminist scholars, among others, increasingly recognize the need to challenge this approach. . . . The myth of objectivity serves to conceal the fact that the male mind has become sacred and is allowed to experiment regardless of the social, human or ecological consequences."[3]

In her Introduction to *The Creation of Patriarchy*, Gerda Lerner adds another layer to the need to remember and retell the goddess tale by saying, "The existence of women's history has been obscured and neglected by patriarchal thought, a fact which has significantly affected the psychology of men and women."[4] These facts that Stone and Condron and Lerner uncovered about Earth's historical past have also obscured truth in the telling of both women's and men's stories.

Merlin Stone believes, however, that those who are descended from the vanished ones can still bring back what is unwritten. She opens her book *When God Was a Woman* with, "In the beginning, people prayed to the Creatress of Life, . . . At the very dawn of religion, God was a woman. Do you remember?"[5] Carol Christ quotes Monique Wittig when she writes, "'There was a time when you [woman] were not a slave, remember that. . . . Make an effort to remember. Or, failing that, invent.'"[6]

Another approach to remembering and retelling lost stories concerns indigenous myths and legends from North American tribes. In 1981, Anne Cameron, a white woman, put into written form the stories of the Nootka people, a people who had never written down their ways, their traditions, and their stories. She did so because she was afraid that the ways of the tribe that had helped her out of her misery as a battered white child would be swallowed up and lost; the loss of their stories would accompany the loss of the tribe.[7]

At a conference called "Telling It, Women and Language Across Cultures," in Vancouver, BC, in November 1988, the indigenous Canadian women asked Anne Cameron to stop using Native culture and stories in her books. *They* want to be the ones who write from their traditions. Even though Cameron wrote the stories as they were told to her, the indigenous women writers believe that she failed to transmit the core of their culture, known only to those who have genetic ties to the tribe; thus, for them, she did not tell the truth. Cameron consented to move aside since now there are indigenous women who have been called by the tribes to preserve the oral traditions in writing.[8]

Indigenous women writers such as Jeanette Armstrong, Carol Lee Sanchez, Leslie Marmon Silko and Paula Gunn Allen believe that only those who are from the tribes can record and critique their stories. They think that non-indigenous do not get the stories right, thereby perpetuating the lies that have kept the indigenous

tribes dependent on white men's laws and at a poverty level that
does not allow them to live in the old ways available to them before
the European conquest.[9]

In the 1989 edition of her book *Spider Woman's Granddaughters*, Paula Gunn Allen writes that she compiled this book of
stories, with permission from the storytellers, in order for the stories "not to be read as 'women's literature' . . . but as tribal women's
literature. . . . I want the reader to understand that tribal women—
who have many differences from and with Indian men, to be sure—
have even greater differences from non-Indian women, particularly
white women."[10] Though the Native American women writers
wanted their stories heard in order to preserve the ways that
worked best for them in the tribes, conflicts arose over who could
tell the stories informed by the truths that the tribes wanted to be
told. According to some of the Native-American women, their
truths were not the truths of the white world.

One reason that many of the stories and traditions have died
out among the indigenous is because written storytelling was foreign to their ways, so when something happened to bring a tribe to
the point of extinction, there would be no written records to keep
the traditions alive. Sun Bear tells the story that during the
Eisenhower administration, the government wanted private industry to develop reservation lands as well as terminate the Bureau of
Indian Affairs. The policies enacted said to the Native Americans:
"You're no longer members of a tribe, because the tribe no longer
exists." The policies did not succeed because Native American
resistance ran high, but not before those *potential* policies worked
to disband a number of tribes, particularly in the Oregon and
Washington State area.[11] In the 1950s, then, through the strategy
of redefinition, several tribes, and thus millions of ancestors and
their stories, became silenced.

In an essay called "Where I Ought to Be: A Writer's Sense of
Place," Louise Erdrich writes that from the mid-fifteenth century
to 1910, the population of Native North Americans shrank from an

estimated 15 million to just over 200,000: from "diseases such as measles and smallpox . . . through a systematic policy of cultural extermination." She believes that for those reasons, "the full magnificence of a variety of Native American cultures were never . . . known by Europeans."[12]

However, ancestral memory and years of research gave Joseph Bruchac hope that the old ways were not extinct but only silenced. Bruchac interviewed over forty Native American poets for his book called *Survival This Way*. He found that Native writers such as Vine Deloria, Gary Hobson and Wendy Rose have logged over two hundred years (from 1772) and three thousand entries of published writings by American Indians. Bruchac also found that though some tribes keep a "lower than low profile" such as the Abenaki people of western Vermont (his tribe), they still remain *Indian*.

What is the theme of these Native American writers? Survival: "personal, . . . of Indian people as a whole, . . . of this planet, this biosphere," interwoven with the motifs of continuance and renewal. They survive through their stories in which the threads of continuance, renewal and survival run strong, and are unbreakable. These threads, passing through the words of poets, have their beginnings in the western definition of pre-history with "roots as deep as the rocks . . . at the very least, thirty thousand years."[13]

As the Native American poets found hard evidence that their ancestors left written records in the United States back to 1772, so, too, have feminist historians discovered written evidence that at one time women were not subservient. Thus women need not "invent" anymore. We can, in truth, remember without the need to invent, "that [we] walked alone, full of laughter . . . bathed barebellied."[14]

Story, according to Jane Yolen, is what affirms humans in their humanity, "not the development of the thumb or the ability to laugh. Stories. They remind us of our past; they force us to the future."[15] Marilyn Sanders Mobley talks of story in similar fashion to Yolen; she writes, "[Story] not only teaches us to value our ancestors but the value of *nommo*—the power of the word—to help us name ourselves and shape our lives in the tradition of our ancestors."[16]

According to Gabriele Lusser Rico, the need to tell stories, or in the verb form, to story, is fundamental to intellectual development. We have, says Rico, an innate drive to create wholeness out of our manifold experience in the form of stories and to express that wholeness to others. As cited by Rico, Renée Fuller writes that this drive occurs at a formative stage of intellectual development, and it occurs in all cultures.

Through storying, we build our sense of who we are and what is significant for our world view. Through storying, we "make mental connections, . . . perceive patterns, . . . create relationships among people, things, feelings and events, . . . and we carry with these drives a need to express these perceived connections to others."[17]

Storytelling gives voice to and articulates what has been silenced, repressed, and excluded in the lives of people of the tribes when the stories that were written down by their oppressors became law. When those laws excluded the way of life of the silenced tribes, the impact was sometimes devastating. The most obvious example is the first of the Ten Commandments: "I am the Lord thy God. Thou shalt not have strange gods before me." Thus the exclusion of the goddess in all of her forms and spirituality became "out" lawed, and any people who were caught performing ceremonies honoring her were punished.[18]

Paula Gunn Allen notes that for Native Americans, storying was an important part of ritual and ceremony. How else were beliefs and attitudes passed on except through story? Leslie Marmon Silko, from the Laguna Pueblo, and a cousin to Paula Gunn Allen, wrote a book called *Storyteller* that she dedicated to: "the storytellers as far back as memory goes and *to the telling* [emphasis mine] which continues and through which all live and we with them."[19] In Silko's sense of "telling" of the story, she emphasizes the importance of the teller communicating to an audience, usually in an oral manner. The telling emphasizes immediacy, dynamism (as opposed to stasis), and interaction and interconnection with another or others: a listener-response experience.

What *is* story? I call on David Leeming's definition because it describes precisely the role that story played in my journey. He defines *story* as the narrating of a sequence of events that helps the reader/listener to "search for identity in the context of the universal struggle between order and chaos."[20] Storytelling answers for me, " who I am and how I came to be" and places me in the vast construct of the cosmos. Thus when I talk of telling stories, the need to tell them and the need to hear or read them, I feel that I am touching the absolute core of human existence, the center of all that I hold sacred as well as profane, the matrix of all that is living and has lived, of life's energy itself. When I tell, or listen to, stories, I am immersing myself in the most profound of all intertextualities: the web of life: (*Whatever we do to the web, we do to ourselves.*) Finding Leeming's definition of story gave me a context for my affinity to the narrative.

When people feel disconnected, stories connect them one to another. Note the renaissance in groups designed to help people by having them tell their stories to receptive others: Alcoholics Anonymous, Overeaters Anonymous, Recovery, Friends of the Bereaved, La Leche League, courses on college campuses that teach students how to be storytellers. These groups provide places for people to tell their stories, knowing that they will be heard in an environment of safety. In *Crow and Weasel* by Barry Lopez, Badger says to Crow and Weasel about stories: "care for them. And learn to give them away when they are needed."[21] Storytellers must be aware of those in their company who need a story. Badger continues, "Sometimes a person needs a story more than food to stay alive. That is why we put these stories in each other's memory."[22]

A fictive storyteller who is a personification of Badger's advice is Granny Oldknow in the five-part Green Knowe series by Lucy Boston. Granny, owner of the mansion and grounds called Green Knowe, is a superb storyteller. She knows when someone needs a story more than food to stay alive, and she has an unending collection of stories. In examining Granny Oldknow as a storyteller, Lynn Rosenthal observes, "Like any good storyteller, Granny Oldknow saves her best stories for moments when she senses that Tolly [one of the children who lives temporarily at Green Knowe] is frightened or lonely. These times often occur when . . . the universe begins to appear disordered and meaningless."[23] Disorder in the human spirit calls up the need for stories in all humans: children and adults.

The stories that Granny Oldknow tells through the series are ones that help her listeners to replace dis-order with order, as principles of an invisible yet influencing order, and as connections between the primordial past, the present, and the future. In so doing, the listeners and the teller (Granny Oldknow) discover their relationship to the universe. "Telling helps me remember" says Granny to Tolly.

For example, in *The Children of Green Knowe*, the first narrative in the five-narrative series, Tolly comes into the mansion called Green Knowe after playing outside for a while. He was particularly distressed by an encounter with a bird. The encounter is not a particularly unpleasant one on the surface, but Tolly comes to Green Knowe a confused and uprooted child: his father and stepmother are in Burma; he was in a boarding school outside of London, and then, suddenly, he was transported to live with his great- grandmother whom he has never met and who is to protect him during the remainder of World War II. Since he has neither a center, nor roots in his life, even a brief encounter with a bird that lands near him in a tree causes him acute distress.

Granny sees him return to the mansion and says to him, "You have been alone quite long enough." She then tells him about his sixteenth-century ancestor Toby and Toby's horse Feste. Feste is a horse with unusual powers; he understands the undercurrents of life and on one occasion saves Toby's life. Feste saving Toby's life is the story that Granny tells Tolly this time. Tolly feels great comfort in hearing about the horse, comfort in the "knowledge that the world into which he was born had once produced a Feste."[24] Tolly is becoming rooted through ancestral stories. He learns that he belongs somewhere and to someone. That feeling of belonging makes him feel safe in the sacred space of Green Knowe.

According to Alice Walker, her parents and grandparents knew stories "to make you weep, or laugh," and telling stories to make one weep or laugh is as important as telling stories that teach lessons, because stories that make one weep or laugh also teach lessons. The stories that made her relatives weep or laugh revealed the joy of knowing that her people were "descendants of an inventive, joyous, courageous, and outrageous people, loving drama, appreciating it, and . . . relishing the pleasure of each other's loquacious and *bodacious* company."[25] Walker is referring to the effect that Zora Neale Hurston's stories had on her relatives.

One time, a long time ago, when the world was new and young, Walker's ancestors knew these stories because they had lived them. She wanted to make certain that these stories stayed in their memories, so she read Hurston's stories aloud to her family: she was afraid that they were becoming assimilated into the dominant white culture of suburbs and plastic furniture, forgetting their Southern, African-American inheritance; forgetting their roots. Her oral reading of Hurston's stories to her family helped them to remember and to reroot themselves in an ancestry that was slipping rapidly from their memory. Through the stories they remembered, and they wept and they laughed, and they were fed.

For Toni Morrison, writing about ancestors is essential in her works; she calls this writing, "the best of that which is female and the best of that which is male. . . . When you kill the ancestor you kill yourself. I want to point out the dangers, to show that nice things don't always happen to the totally self-reliant if there is no conscious historical connection."[26]

There is another aspect to storytelling that has intrigued me for a long time and has not been given a lot of lengthy attention when *story* is described and analyzed. Usually when we hear the word "story," most likely we think of a parent reading or telling a child something that begins with, "Once upon a time." Or, as someone involved with literary form, oftentimes my first thoughts are, "plot, characters, narrator." However, in doing research for this study, I was brought up short in the moment that I realized that storying is more than oral or written word-telling. It includes all articulations of experiences that narrate, even the ones that narrate non-verbally. Some non-verbal narratives are found in music, mime, sculpture, painting, gardens, needlework, and the various sub-categories of these larger experiences. I will detail two of these forms: needlework and gardens.

Two of my hobbies, if you will, are gardening and needlework. Until recently I was unaware that in both can be seen wonderfully complex and articulate tales. I admit to my lately-learned insight with some embarrassment simply because I have been involved with both of those storytelling aspects for decades without being fully conscious of what they were telling me. My literal voice was silenced early-on, so, besides retreating to the woods near my home, I turned to gardening and needleworking to find ways to create and connect with something beyond myself that was non-threatening to those around me.

However, it was my lack of attention to the Earth's non-verbal guides that has brought me to this point in my life where, with a single-minded will and purpose, I have delved as deeply as I can into the unknown of the cosmos to unravel the reasons behind the uprootedness that has been controlling my existence. So although the insight to consciousness surprised me, upon reflection I saw it as another signpost that I had neglected to recognize for years in my attempt to keep pace with the rules of the game played out by the society in which I live.

Neither gardening nor needlework come to mind immediately when one asks for non-verbal examples of storytelling, and yet both are deeply embedded in the historical memory of all human beings. Needles for sewing, made from bone, are found among ancient remnants of indigenous tribes. Gardening has been with us since agriculture replaced the hunter-gatherer way of life. Non-verbal storytelling in gardening and needlework is taken for granted; it is seen as background.

Background has difficulty being acknowledged, because part of the nature of background is its silence, its non-verbal quality, in a culture that places words and their uses in print and verbal media as a priority. When Rozsika Parker did extensive and thorough research on the history of embroidery—a form of needlework—in England and the United States, she discovered that "knowing the history of embroidery is to know the history of women," because both embroidery and women have been background, taken for granted.[27] She discovered that in the Middle Ages, women worked alongside men in embroiderers' guild workshops, but by the nineteenth century, stitchery had become "both symbol and instrument of female subservience."[28] Recently, she discovered, groups of women have used embroidery as a symbol to demonstrate resistance. During the Suffrage Movement in Great Britain, groups of suffragettes embroidered banners with slogans and faces that celebrated the achievements of well-known women, "knowing full well the story they were telling—the story of women's oppression in Western civilization."[29]

These suffragettes also made a banner embroidered with the names of the women leaders who were force-fed in jail. Notes Parker, "the banner transformed a prison gesture of solidarity into a public statement."[30] The personal was made political through needlework, a non-verbal storytelling form. The women at

Greenham Common Air Base embroider banners and attach them to the fence that encloses the air base. Parker discovered in interviewing the women responsible for the banners that it is their way of campaigning against nuclear threat *as women*. The women at Greenham Common, then, use a culturally endowed feminine resource to make a public and political statement.

Parker fills readers with the insight that this non-verbal storytelling form, once intended to "inculcate self-effacement, piety and passivity in women" has been turned back on the dominant culture to become a source of quiet strength as embroiderers have entered the public, political and artistic spheres.

In 1979, Judy Chicago was one of those who brought embroidery back to its origins of artistic equality with her needlework project called The Dinner Party. In "Creating a Work of Art," from her book called *The Dinner Party*, which documents the process involved in creating the art work, Chicago tells why she decided to use embroidery as an integral part of the work: "to aggrandize women, relating our history through the varieties of needlework women have traditionally used . . . and [to] honor yet another female tradition."[31] This work tells the stories of thirty-nine women in myth and history, from Primordial Goddess through Macha and Sojourner Truth to Georgia O'Keeffe.

Thirty friends of feminist theologian Nelle Morton surprised her with a friendship quilt in 1984. It made Morton pause to reflect that quilting is helping to recover personal history as well as making a political statement: "It represents the powerful bonding of women and fierce tenderness of woman friendship."[32] In the mid-eighties when Morton published her book, she believed that quiltmaking was partially replacing the early consciousness-raising groups; it was that important as a way to express one's story.

Beth Brant discusses another facet of needlework as storytelling. Brant is half Mohawk, half white; she writes from her Mohawk ancestry, working arduously to preserve her specific tribal culture, particularly the women's role in the tribe. In her book

Mohawk Trail, she narrates that her aunts all married white men, then quit their jobs upon marrying. However, they did more than keep the house clean: "they became secret artists, putting up huge amounts of quilts, needlework and beadwork in the fruit cellars . . . By day, the dutiful wife. By night, sewing and beading their souls into beauty that will be left behind after their death, telling the story of who these women were."[33]

Keeping the work in the fruit cellars, no matter how beautiful the work, tells me, as reader of this experience, that these women, too, like the ones in England, stitched their work subversively; they knew that their husbands would not enter the fruit cellars. A fruit cellar is a woman's place. It is where the jars of vegetables and fruits are stored for the winter after they have been preserved, or "put up." Not only did these women stitch, a silent way to tell a story, they stitched as "secret artists."

Art, however, is not meant to be "secret." Art is an outpouring of and by a soul seeking a connection. Thus, in my mind, "secret artists" is a phrase in contradiction; as a contradiction, it says that these women were desperate to tell their story through an artistic medium—needlework—yet faced with a reality that if the art work were discovered, they feared it would be destroyed. If it were destroyed, so would their soul's Self that storied the connection be destroyed. In a word, a secret artist is a silenced artist. I was sad when I read about these secret artists because the phrase made me realize that women's stories, ideas, and creativity still are not accepted in our society. Whenever there is fear to express, in whatever form, it means that the threat of violence to the Self is dominant. And it also means that sacred spaces are not open, communal spaces, but hidden ones like fruit cellars.

Paula Gunn Allen explains about tribal narratives and women's lives by using the image of quilting. Allen relates that the form of tribal narratives are the most difficult aspect of her culture to explain to her non-Indian readers, because tribal narratives and white narratives stand in opposition to and isolation from one another. She finds that the two ways of narrating are antithetical to each other. First, Native American narratives in their purity of origins are oral, so "any typeset version of traditional materials is distorting." Second, she sees that "conventions of literacy militate against an understanding of traditional tribal materials." Allen says that the distance from conventional literary tradition is true of all folk and tribal literature as well as the literature of women, "who, after all, inhabit a separate folk tradition." Thus the gap is wide between the ways of storytelling.

She tries to close the gap by explaining that women's literature and philosophies and tribal literature and philosophies, as well as their arts and crafts, "are more often accretive than linear, more achronological than chronological, and more dependent on harmonious relationships of all elements within a field of perception than western culture in general."[34]

To help clarify her point, she tells about Native American women and the quilt: in particular, the patchwork quilt. Quilting is a non-Indian woman's craft/art; however, when taught to the Native American women, they take to it "avidly," relates Allen, and they display their finished works in ceremonies and in their homes. Allen's point is that, like women's stories, the patchwork quilt is accretive, achronological, and dependent on harmonious relationship, as is the plot and process of a traditional tribal narrative.

The most contemporary example of needlework as storytelling is the AIDS quilt that is now touring the United States. It is a work that moves audiences to tears. On July 11, 1992, ABC aired a two-hour special that presented the latest information on AIDS. The entire quilt was displayed; several of the panels and the stories behind the deaths of the persons who inspired the making of the panels were given extra time on the show. One of the show's hosts, Robert Guillaume, showed the panel dedicated to his son, a young singer, dead of AIDS. This quilt, a patchwork quilt, definitely shows the "plot and process of a traditional tribal narrative." The "plot and process" is the killing off of millions of people by HIV that leads to AIDS; the "tribe" I call "the Earth's people."

When I was in San Francisco in August 1992, I visited the storefront that houses the AIDS quilt, and though the quilt had been disassembled and placed on shelves, the power that it gave off when I entered the store hit me as forcefully as if someone had pushed me.

The whole quilt contains thousands of individual panels. Each panel tells the story of a person who died from AIDS. The panels are sewn into 12' x 12' blocks. When displayed in public, the blocks are then laid out into the artwork called "the AIDS quilt." The quilt is accretive, achronological and "dependent on harmonious relationships of all elements within a field of perception," and, until no one ever dies of AIDS again, it will never be finished; it will grow panel by panel, block by block, sewn together by volunteers in San Francisco. The AIDS victims, the survivors of the victims who create the panels, the volunteers who sew the panels into blocks, and AIDS itself are all tellers of a very powerful—and truthful— story titled "AIDS."

Using needlework as a non-verbal clue to tell a story is a technique that turn-of-the-century fiction writer Susan Glaspell uses in her narrative titled "A Jury of Her Peers." The story is set in a small farming community in Iowa in the early 1900s. Three men— a sheriff named Mr. Peters, a country attorney named Henderson and a farmer, Mr. Hale— are called to a farmhouse where Minnie Foster Wright has allegedly killed her husband, John. They go to search for clues that will identify her as the murderer. The wives of the sheriff and the farmer, Mrs. Peters and Mrs. Hale, accompany them.

The clue that identifies Minnie as the perpetrator is found in the quilt on which she was working. Most of the quilt pieces had fine, even sewing but for one: "Why it looks as if she didn't know what she was about!" said Mrs. Hale. "The difference was startling. Holding this block made Mrs. Hale feel nervous, as if the distracted thoughts of the woman who had perhaps turned to it to try and quiet herself were communicating themselves to her."[35]

The uneven sewing of the one patch was indeed communicating itself to Mrs. Hale. It told of the sewer's agitated state of mind after her husband had killed her canary by wringing its neck, and she, then, killed her husband by wringing *his* neck—she hung him with a rope while he slept. The motive for the killing was communicated to the women by non-verbal clues they found in the kitchen: the uneven sewing, the dead canary, the broken door on the canary's bird cage. The three men found no evidence of motive because they were looking for "awful important things" in the bedroom where the killing took place, and in the barn. Of course they found nothing, because the evidence was among the "lesser" things, "woman" things, invisible to the men because the clues were in the kitchen.

Gardens also tell non-verbal stories especially for and about, although not confined to, women. Annette Kolodny wrote a landmark text called *The Land Before Her: Fantasy and Experience of the American Frontiers, 1630-1860.* I will merely touch on one issue that Kolodny covers in this study and recommend that the entire book be read to savor her insight and her scholarship. The specific area that I will dip into is the meaning that gardens held for the frontier women that Kolodny uncovered in her research. Her sources are women's diaries and novels from 1630–1860.

The major point she makes is that gardens planted on the frontier helped those women to establish visible roots in their new communities. The women hoped to heal the wrenching of their lives from the established communities where they were born and raised by the planting of the gardens in their new communities. For many of these women, gardening was an attempt to turn the unfamiliar landscape into a kind of mother bestowing "lavish love"; the women "experience a psychic rebirth" because they use the gardens as a symbol of childhood mothering. Repossessing "the maternal garden of childhood . . . the women healed the trauma of the rural nightmare" imposed by their uprooting.[36] It was Margaret Crane Fuller who expressed this parallel between mothers and gardens in her diary; however, it was a parallel that applied to almost every frontier woman of whom Kolodny wrote.

The men were the ones who had wanted to move west, "and the women followed, as women will, doing their best for affection's sake."[37] According to Kolodny, the men's fantasies were American Adam fantasies: "savages to conquer, trees to plow up." The frontier was their "invitation for mastery and possession of the vast new continent, with all its concomitant psycho-sexual associations."[38]

The frontier claimed many of these women in childbirth, raids, and a plain harshness they were unprepared for. Planting and harvesting the garden *and the writing about* the planting and harvesting of it, were very important in sustaining the sanity of many of the women; the garden told the women of their ties to the community they left behind. Seeds from the flowers that grew in their gardens in New York could be planted in their gardens in Michigan. Then the stories could be told to other frontier women of the history of these seeds, the remembrances.

In the fall of 1990, *The Amicus Journal* published an essay by Sallie Bingham titled "A Woman's Land." In her essay, Bingham expresses an idea about gardens: "Generally we [women] are not farmers, but gardeners."[39]

Bingham purchased a piece of land—too large for a garden— that created in her a need to philosophize on the nature of gardens/farms/land. The land spoke to Bingham by telling her that "it" does not need her to exist: "The land is given only to itself—it exists for me as does the ground under my feet, but not as a possibility, a future, a hope of gain."

Owning land brings her to form a theory, like Kolodney's, that whoever owns the land will decide how the land is to be used. She finds that women who own land do not exploit it, "even in situations where exploitations is possible or expected." Men who own land she calls "land-patriarchs" because in her experience she finds that men want land for profit and gain. The only male who does not want to turn a profit is the male artist, she says, "unless their androgyny is corrupted by power and money." She includes her husband and sons among the land patriarchs who will take over the land she owns one day and, she reflects, will sell it for housing tracts or malls.

Ben Logan believes that the land in any size and dimension dialogues with those who work with it. This belief he puts in his memoir called *The Land Remembers, the story of a farm and its people*. The farm and its people live in southwestern Wisconsin, near Aldo Leopold country, near my country. It is his remembrance of garden-land that I want to delve into here.

Logan makes the distinction that he, his father, brothers, and hired hand plowed, planted and homesteaded the fields of one hundred acres while his mother plowed and planted her garden. Thus what I see in Logan's book is a lived experience by one family in the 1920s, '30s and '40s of the research of Annette Kolodny and the observations of Sallie Bingham. The difference in Kolodny's research and Bingham's observations from Logan's experience is in the attitude of the Logan men to the land: they did not plow to conquer and possess, but to grow food to live by; they were "partners with its moods, secrets, and seasons . . . asking the oats if tomorrow is the day harvest should begin."[40]

Unlike the frontier women, Logan's mother was born in the hill country where they farmed. Like the frontier women, her garden gave her rootedness to the land; the garden's growth showed her that she and the land lived in a symbiotic relationship. As with the field-land, her garden-land told her when it was ready to receive the seeds. Logan's mother believed that the seeds grew well in her garden because "Each seed passed through the warmth of our hands . . . into the soil so they could awake and grow." As the youngest child, Ben Logan helped with the garden in his early years; thus he, too, planted the dahlia roots that his mother had dug up in the fall of the previous year where, until the next spring they lay dormant in the cellar, "dead-looking clumps, dried roots from last year"; and gladiolus bulbs, dug up and preserved the same way as the dahlia roots, "heavy but with no sign of growth." (Dahlias and gladioli will freeze and die if left in the ground in Wisconsin over winter.) But the gladiolus and the dahlia grew along with the rest of the garden that the mother planted year after year, because the new growth was inside, invisible to human eyes, safe from probing fingers that may be tempted to force its maturing, its bloom.

Ben's mother died the winter he was sixteen: "The winter, the same winter that always killed her fall flowers and sent her birds away, caused her death."[41] He found it hard to come to terms with the loss, because it was so unexpected. She had fallen on ice, broken her leg, and died a few weeks later when a blood clot, released by the accident, hit her heart.

The following spring Ben and Lyle, the hired man, prepared to plant the garden: "following the pattern of other years . . . the mysterious living seeds passed through my fingers, one by one." After planting, Ben climbed the white pine tree near the house and started to cry because he realized that the story the garden told him was, "I had not entirely lost her after all. The seeds germinated. Neat rows of new green pushed up in the garden. The land remembers."[42]

Another memoir that relates the storytelling nature of gardens is *Getting Home Alive*, written by Rosario Morales and Aurora Levins Morales. Aurora, the daughter, learns about gardens from her great-grandmother, Leah, who told her that "you can make a garden anywhere, with anything, anyone . . . . always to plant [. . .] then always you have a garden." Aurora's great-grandmother stretched the meaning and nature of garden from planting seeds in earth to growing children, making a home. They too were gardens to her: "you want to know gardens? Let me show you gardens!" In expanding the meaning of *gardens*, her great-grandmother could have gardens even in the section of Brooklyn where she had no soil to plant a literal one. It is through the planting of literal and metaphorical gardens that Aurora communicates with Leah, now dead, when she says to her in monologue: "I was torn from the moist soil of Indiera, roots ripping, and transplanted to stony ground. I have dug myself carefully up and planted myself here. You would be proud of me, Leah. I have finally learned to make gardens."[43]

Probably the most famous of all gardens is the secret garden in the narrative by Frances Hodgsen Burnett bearing the same title, first published in 1911. It is a garden that lay dormant for years, behind high stone walls and under lock and key. It lay dormant since the untimely death of the wife of the master of the manor. The master of the manor locked up the garden when his wife died because the garden had been his wife's, and he wanted nothing to remind him of her. Her death had taken with it his spirit and reason to find joy in life.

This particular garden is found and transformed into a living being by two children. One is Mary, the niece of the master, sent to live with him when her parents died of the plague in India. The other is Dickon, a boy rooted in Earth's ways, who lives in the area of the manor and talks to animals. He shows Mary how to rebirth the garden.

A major part of the story is the telling of the effects the garden has on them, as well as the people they come to know. The blooming of the garden parallels the blooming of Mary, who when she arrived from India was a disagreeable and unlikable little girl, and Colin, the master's son, shut up in a castle room with an imaginary illness in order to be kept from the sight of his father. The son, like the garden, reminds the father of his dead wife. The garden, in its silence, has been waiting for the children to participate in the process needed to transform itself and, in particular, Mary and Colin. Contact with the earth through the garden gives new life to these children, and before the story concludes, the father.

Sarah learns about the importance of gardens, too. Sarah is a woman who leaves her birth-and-growing-up place in Maine in the latter part of the nineteenth century to be a mother to two young motherless children in Kansas. Patricia MacLaughlin tells Sarah's story in her Newbery award-winning book called *Sarah, Plain and Tall*. The corn fields and prairie grass of Kansas, with no water to speak of nearby, are totally foreign to Sarah, reared in a Maine coastal fishing village. She does her best to adjust, but she finds it difficult. One day in spring, her only neighbors within eye's view, Matthew and Maggie, come to help Caleb, the father of the children, plow up a new field for corn. In the back of the buckboard, along with a sackful of live chickens Maggie has brought for Sarah, she brings, "'Plants . . . for your garden.'" "'My garden?'" asks Sarah. "'You must have a garden. Wherever you are'" (Maggie comes from Tennessee). "Sarah smiled. 'I had a garden in Maine with dahlias and columbine. And nasturtiums the color of the sun when it sets. I don't know if nasturtiums would grow here.' 'Try,' said Maggie. 'You must have a garden.'"[44]

Indeed, dahlias and columbine and nasturtiums grow in Maine and in Wisconsin, in upstate New York and in Kansas, because the land knows and remembers how to grow and produce its own kind in a bioregion that will accept the seeds and the roots.

Alice Walker goes in search of her mother's gardens both literally and metaphorically. She finds that her mother is an artist, a creator, only after others discover this. What the others discover is that her mother is an artist in growing a garden: "a garden so brilliant with colors . . . that to this day people drive by our house in Georgia . . . and ask to stand or walk among my mother's art," She discovers that "[g]uided by my heritage of a love of beauty and a respect for strength," in search of her mother's garden she finds her own. "Garden" becomes the way the universe speaks to Walker's creative literary spark, bringing her to pen and paper to write of her heritage that is her strength.[45]

The land that becomes a garden has always been important to me, too. One of my most vivid childhood memories about garden land centers on the potatoes we grew every year. My family had a root cellar in the basement of our house where we stored potatoes we had grown that year. We grew enough potatoes to last us until spring of the following year with the last of the crop, having sprouted eyes, saved to plant in order to grow the next crop.

A root cellar itself is an interesting phenomenon. It has a dirt floor; the dirt (the earth) keeps the moisture in balance, something that the potatoes need in order to winter well. If there is a barrier between earth and potatoes, such as a brick or cement floor, or even if the potatoes are suspended by mesh screens, as with garlic and onions, the potatoes will lose their moisture, wither prematurely, and the family will lose their potato crop. So potatoes and earth work in a symbiotic relationship from the time they are planted until the time the family gathers them from the root cellar to eat.

When harvesting potatoes, one digs down into the soil with a fork. And they are always there, waiting, waiting in the dark, cool silence of that soil with the ever-present worms, waiting to be dug up, put in the buckets, then stored in the root cellar until they are needed during the course of winter. *"Take and eat of this,"* said Earth to us, *"for this is from my body. Eat of this and know life everlasting."*

That the land as well as the sea, the sun, the moon and the stars speak to humans is an accepted truth for many Earth-based peoples (as opposed to heaven/sky-based peoples). For Earth-based peoples, what the elements tell us is truth. However, that truth is not shared by all.

Carol Snow, of the Seneca Nation, poet, artist, and zoologist, writes a poem called "The Winter Dreams of Bears." It is true (a fact?) that bears hibernate. "Not so," tells Carol. "They say that bears sleep in winter [. . .]/ they say that the heartbeat slows . . . they say that bears are defined by . . . what they eat, . . . 'this is bear' . . . they are only partly right./ we know that Bears leave the forms They wear, . . . we hear the Bears' voices disguised in winter breath. . . ./ we know Their chants of power in the sound of ice cracking/ . . . Medicine Bears . . ./ Spirit Bears . . ./ they say that bears awaken in spring . . ./ We know that Bears never sleep."[46]

"Not so. Bears sleep in winter," says a doubting Thomas. "Maybe the bears you know sleep, but the Bears that I know don't" would answer Carol Snow. "You're making that up. That's not true. Experts who study bears know what's true. So you can't be right." The doubting Thomas wants an either/or answer to a question that seems foolish to ask in the first place. The one known as "we" sees that bears hibernate *and* that Bears never sleep.

Here the reader/listener is confronted with who is telling the truth, with what *is* the truth, what is *the* truth, and with what is *truth*. All of these questions and the issues they raise are important in storytelling.

If we look more closely at the poem by Carol Snow, we will find clues that answer some of these questions. Snow has distinctions for two different spirits of bears: for one, she uses the lower case *b*, for the other, the upper case *B*. When she speaks of the bears that the doubting Thomas knows of, she uses the lower case letter. These are the bears that hibernate in winter. The assumption that bears hibernate in winter and awaken in the spring is centered on the idea that bears live only on a physical plane. Thus when those-who-study-bears check the bears' caves in the winter time, they find those bears asleep.

However, Carol Snow tells us that though bears live on a physical plane, "they [bear checkers] are only partly right." Bears, upper case B, also live on a spirit plane. Upper-case B Bears "leave the form They wear." They do not need their bodies; They are "unshaped by physical desires." These are the Bears that "walk through our winter dreams . . . and when They let us see them . . ./ we know the truths of Ourselves."[47]

Those who do not believe in the spirit plane, or that animals contain spirit power that can fill heart "with crystal knowledge" will not believe that there are bears and there are Bears, that "bears awaken in spring" and "Bears never sleep." Carol Snow even sets up the dialectic with "they say" and "we know," so she accepts that there is a group of people who will not believe as truth that Bears carry spirit power and thus never sleep. The words *truth, the truth,* and even *truths,* then, are defined differently for the two groups of people who seem to be observing the same reality. Carol Snow has looked at the divergent realities, the reality of dualism and the reality of continuance and harmony as she ends her poem: "they say that bears awaken in spring. . . . We know that Bears never sleep."[48]

Is it true, as Paula Gunn Allen says it is, that Native American tribes were women-centered until the Conquest? Was the Earth viewed as gynocentric? Does it matter? It matters very much to women of the tribes, to Allen and Silko, and Beth Brant and Joy Harjo and Linda Hogan, and Gail Tremblay. It also matters to Lorraine Anderson, a white woman, who wrote in the Preface to her anthology *Sisters of the Earth*: "I've adopted the metaphor of [E]arth as female in naming the themes I've grouped my writing around. . . . I've . . . used the metaphor because it has . . . historical import, having been used by varied cultures throughout the ages."[49]

Allen, Sanchez, and Silko explores that "truth" of women-centeredness in Native American tribes, researching their material back beyond the written records to include the traditions passed down orally through their ancestors to them as members of the Laguna Pueblo people, people who can remember a gynocentered culture.

Gail Tremblay, Onondaga, wrote a poem with the same truth and called it "After the Invasion": "On dark nights, the women cry together/. . . talking to their Grandmother Moon/ about the way life got confused. . . . Women murmur about men who don't sing/

when women grind the corn . . .—defeat makes them forget/ to see the magic when women dance. . . . They weep for sisters who have learned to hate,/ who have gone crazy and learned to hurt/ the fragile web that makes people whole./ Together, women struggle to remember how to live."[50]

The theme: at one time, before the conquest/invasion, tribes were women-centered, ritual and ceremony were vital to those tribes, men did not "drink and make lewd remarks," the incidence of rape and abuse was almost non-existent, and some Native women, to this day, remember how it was.[51] In their ancestral memory is the truth, fact, that not only were their tribes women-centered, they were non-violent.

"Not so," that doubting Thomas would cry. "Look at the research on Natives that says otherwise." "The research is wrong," says Allen.[52] Paula Gunn Allen and Gail Tremblay are two of the many voices joining to correct a false claim that has been repeated for five hundred years in written research and documentation. These Native Americans, however, do not define written literacy as a condition for right living. What they do define as a priority is not harming Earth, because they recognize that Earth gives them life through the food grown and, in death, a place to rest their bodies.

Allen, Tremblay, Brant, Hogan, Harjo, Silko do not say that no Native never committed a wrongdoing before the invasion by the Europeans. They did, and there were ways to reprimand those who did. Most Native tribes include in their storytelling tales of the Trickster, a clown of either gender or an animal that forces people to see themselves as others see them at times when they act inappropriately to the way of the tribe. For the Iroquois those disrupting the life of the tribe would have to appear before the Mothers of the Longhouse. The central authority of the people rested with the Mothers. They even had the power to impeach the sachems, or leaders, of the clans, should they prove derelict in carrying out their duties as envisioned by the Mothers and set forth by the Law of the Great Peace of the Iroquois Confederacy.[53] Mariliou Awiakta reinforces the evidence of Allen's research with a story that begins her tale called "Amazons in Appalachia": "Where are your women?"

> The speaker is Attakullakulla, a Cherokee chief renowned for his shrewd and effective diplomacy. He has come to negotiate a treaty with the whites. Among his delegation are women "as famous in war as powerful in the Council." Their presence also has ceremonial significance: it is meant to show honor to the other delegation. But that delegation is composed of males only. To them the absence of their women is irrelevant, a trivial consideration. To the Cherokee, however, reverence for women/ Mother Earth/life/spirit is interconnected. Irreverence for one is likely to mean irreverence for all. Implicit in their chief's question, "Where are your women?" the Cherokee hear, "Where is your balance? What is your intent?" They see that the balance is absent and are wary of the white men's motives. They intuit the mentality of destruction.[54]

Where is the truth? A useful compromise is to say that the truth lies somewhere in-between one side and the other. But is "in-between" the truth? Alice Walker says that, "in-between" means "half": "half-perceived, half-rendered 'truths.'" In the mid-seventies, she spoke of the books in print that do not tell the truth about black people; books "less valuable, if more 'profitable,' survive to insult us," while books of "the black women writers and poets go out of print."[55]

In July 1992, in an interview with the Associated Press at a Manhattan hotel she said: "There are white writers who can write as if they're in America and there aren't Native American or black people. . . . It's really hard to read those books, because when I open one up it seems so unreal to me,"[56] Walker raises another issue that is important in developing theory on storytelling; she claims that stories that lack multi-cultural diversity in a nation like America that is, by definition, multi-culturally diverse, lack truth and authenticity.

Barry Lopez finds truth in storytelling to be a crucial issue. In "Landscape and Narrative," a section in his book called *Crossing Open Ground*, he spills many words to explain his view clearly. He explains, first, the importance of integrating our outer and inner landscapes because our inner landscape "responds to the character and subtlety of an exterior landscape; the shape of the individual mind is affected by land as it is by genes." He states that the listener is satisfied with a story when "he has heard something pleasing and authentic—trustworthy."[57] He says that "We derive this sense of confidence . . . not so much from *verifiable truth* [emphasis mine] as from an understanding that *lying* has played no role in the narrative." Both phrases involve a presence or absence of integrity between the language, details and incidents that mesh the inner landscape of the characters in the narrative with the outer landscape of place or setting. Therefore, in this context, to Lopez, lying would be not relating the balance of those two landscapes.

Though he is not a Navajo, Lopez has studied and lived with the Navajo, and he integrates the Navajo way into his theories on narrative. He reports that to the Navajos, the land, or landscape, exhibits a sacred order. *Land* is defined as "the universe." The way the Navajos seek to achieve a balanced state of mental health is to succeed in ordering their interior landscape according to their exterior landscape.

Therefore, if one of the main purposes in storytelling, says Lopez, is to order that balance, lying—willfully not recreating the balance of the order found in all creation—would be a violation of the trust that the listener has placed in the storyteller.

Valerie Andrews agrees with Barry Lopez's concept of inner and outer landscape as he views it from the eyes of the Navajos. She writes:

> Landscape . . is a revelation of the Self and a key to our own moods and inner changes. . . . The earth contains a blueprint of the human psyche, a map of our innate character. It is as accurate an

indicator of who we are as the narrow-ribboned chromosomes that determine our intelligence and genetic sensitivities.[58]

Lopez also speaks directly to the confusion over what constitutes "the truth" in his observation that some people call only non-fiction the truth. He includes all narratives. I concur that all narratives are capable of containing the truth, truth, and/or truths. The distinction between non-fiction and fiction comes from defining *the truth* only as facts gathered from data and observation. We know, for example, from Carol Snow's poem on bears that data and observation can be skewed because data and observation are derived from the point of view of the data collectors and the observers.

For example, a data collector would never agree with Toni Morrison when she says that, "Water has roots, too. . . . What people call 'floods,' water calls 'remembering.' Remembering where it used to be. All water has a perfect memory and is forever trying to get back to where it was."[59] She continues that the reason we have floods is because people try to change the course of rivers and oceans to develop areas for housing, and, like salmon, water has a built-in obligation to return to its roots.

On his dedication page to *The Land Remembers*, Ben Logan tells a story that defines *not* lying:

> Laurance, Lee and Lyle, the only ones left who shared that hill-top world with me, will tell me next time we meet that I didn't get all my facts straight. We'll argue some about that, but mostly I'll just remind them of what a neighbor used to say—"When you're trying to tell somebody who ain't been there just how hot it is in a hayfield with the temperature at a hundred degrees in the shade, it's not lying if you make it a hundred and ten."[60]

Says Lopez, the authentic, the truthful narratives are "rooted in the local landscape." To violate that connection is to call the narrative itself into question." *The Land Remembers* would not be called into question. Narratives called into question would be the tales of Native American life after the conquest as told by Indo-European data collectors.

For Barry Lopez as for Lucy Boston, the power of the narrative is to nurture and to heal, to repair a spirit in disarray, "to reorder a state of psychological confusion through contact with the pervasive truth of those relationships we call 'the land.'"[61] In order to do that well, then, the sources of the narrative must be unimpeachable and the listener must know that "no hypocrisy is involved." I would add: the *narrator* must be reliable. One might say that the narrator's role is implied in the other two; however, "sources" could imply only history of ancestry and listener. "No hypocrisy" could imply that the *content* is integrated. Thus I see a need to mention the narrator, through whose mouth/pen/ needle/brush/ knife/seed planting/ceremony/ritual, truths are being transmitted, because that narrator is the means by which the order of the universe is communicated. I cannot stress enough the need to be aware of whether a narrator is reliable or unreliable, for myths and legends built on unreliability can destroy species and places. Lies and their effects in our lives reveal this truth.

Lopez is not finished with the importance of the thread truthtelling has as it is woven into the strand of storytelling. He says that truth "is something alive and unpronounceable" and in story, "it becomes discernible as a pattern." Lying, then "is the opposite of story for it means that the storyteller "insist[s] on relationships that do not exist." Insists. If the storyteller is telling the truth, then there is no need for insisting, because teller and tale will be in harmony, in balance, in "Beautyway" to use the Navajo word.

Finding the path to healing and wholeness is what the Navajos call Beautyway, and Beauty is "that irreducible, holy complexity that manifests itself as all things changing through time."[62] Recreating that same order in the individual is the Beautyway ceremony. In a story, the inner and outer landscapes would be integrated in the truths that come through the tools of the storyteller to create balance and order for the listener/reader: to nurture and to heal.

Annie Kahn, a Navajo Medicine Woman in Arizona on the Navajo Reservation, describes the path as "I walk in beauty. To walk in beauty is obedience. . . . It is doing things in the right way at the right time. It is order. It is the spring before summer. . . . It is respect for self, because self is nature, is harmonious with the universe."[63]

Annie Kahn substantiates what Lopez describes as the Navajo ways of achieving balance. She says that, "You are sick when you develop the habit of excluding." Her word "exclude" is parallel to Lopez's word "lying." She goes on: "You are off balance. You are out of harmony. . . . There is a shiny crust on some people, like locusts leave. A Shell. . . . Emptiness. It is illness at its worst. . . . When we do not communicate [through the heart], we are ill." Communication includes earth with the sky, people with the universe, the landscape.

For Lopez, the stories need to carry with them one more thing: "paradox, irony, and contradictions that distinguish compelling narratives." In using paradox, irony, and contradictions, "the truth reveals itself most fully." Otherwise we have "reductionism in science, fundamentalism in religion, fascism in politics, not literature that will nurture, sustain, and heal us in its telling."

Lopez stands as a representative of what he says about narrators: "they don't have to know everything in order to be good narrators, but they do need to speak 'the truth.'" Representative of his theory is his story *Crow and Weasel* in which he takes the two characters, Crow and Weasel, on a journey. They take a physical journey, from their home to a land where no one of their tribe has ever gone; they also follow an inner journey as, by story's end, they find wisdom and truth in their experiences . . . a wisdom and truth that they bring back to their people in the form of stories.

Mary Austin, an early twentieth-century American writer, found that the exterior landscape of the desert gave her "the courage to sheer off what is not worthwhile."[64] What was not worthwhile to Austin was anything that was not true, particularly stories that had been told to her in her "civilized upbringing" in order to keep her docile.

In 1990, for Terry Tempest Williams, the exterior landscape of the desert was a home to be reclaimed after men in government had brought slow, painful deaths to many of its inhabitants through unscrupulous atom bomb testing in that desert in the 1950s, '60s and '70s. To both of these writers, living over half a century apart, the desert was home, "soul-centered and strong," for whom the "sweet smell of sage" fueled their spirits and the "tireless spaces uncramp the soul."

Terry Tempest Williams is a storyteller who was born and raised and still lives in Navajoland—Utah. "Each of us harbors a homeland," she writes in *Pieces of White Shell*, and she believes that it is in this homeland that we find our truth, which she equates with Self, her inner being. Thus the exterior landscape of the desert helps her connect to her interior landscape she calls truth, home, Self.

One of her stories that shows the importance of knowing one's homeland is about a Native boy whom everyone thought was retarded. He had been sent to one of the boarding schools for Natives run by whites. The officials sent him home as a failure. He went to a Native school, "where he learned who he was." He eventually became president of the student council. When he learned the truth of his ancestry, his roots, that ancestral truth freed him to be "who he was." When he was grounded in the security of his truth, then he could fly like the eagle to follow his vision and lead his people.

Conscious that she is a non-Indian telling Indian stories, she asks Herb Blatchford, a Navajo holy man, if it is acceptable for her as a non-Indian to use the Indian stories she uncovers in order "to illustrate a land ethic." His answer: "That is why they were created." He is not offended by her desire; he tells her that others may be offended because "some have deeper knowledge than others." That deeper knowledge is greater understanding of creatures' relationships to Earth. Thus some truths, like some rivers, are more complex. He gives her no more explanation, nor does he delineate who has deeper knowledge or what that knowledge is in Indian tradition.

However, he points out to Tempest Williams the difference between Indians' and non-Indians' approach to animals. In Anglo tradition, he says, animals are not "mystified," are not recognized as spirit carriers as they are in the tradition of land-based tribes; therefore, some Anglo stories tell lies about animals. Tempest Willliams gives the example of "Little Red Riding Hood" and "The Three Little Pigs." The actions of the wolves in those stories "are not inherent to wolfness." Therefore, in the words of Barry Lopez, they are not stories. They do not balance our inner and outer worlds.

Another question that Tempest Williams considers in her search for truth through storying and that I described previously from Alice Walker's writings was: how do we swim in the dangerous space of cross-cultural waters? Tempest Williams' answer: we need to look at our own reflection in those waters, see who *we* are, and then right our relationship with Earth by taking time to experience that relationship through direct involvement. After that, we will tell only stories that are true.

Terry Tempest Williams published those thoughts in 1987. In 1991 she published another book called *Refuge* in which she speaks of a hard lesson that gave her "deeper knowledge" about the land from her own non-Indian ancestry, about who she was, and about her connection between land, ancestry, and being. In *Refuge* she wrote of two "facts": 1) the flooding of the Great Salt Lake in the fall of 1986 and winter of 1986–87; and 2) her mother's death from breast cancer in 1987 at the age of fifty-one. The truth told through her mother's death is more than about her mother. It is about "the fact" that at thirty-four, Terry was the eldest woman in her clan. Her mother, two grandmothers, and six aunts all had had mastectomies; seven of the ten dead of the cancer. A genetic deficiency? No, that was not the truth the story told: death came from radiation fallout when in the 1950s the United States government used parts of the Western desert as a testing site for atomic bombs—dozens and dozens of times. The government's rationale was that the desert held "'low-use segments of the population.'"[65] What was implied in the documentation and data collecting was that: 1) Earth is not sacred, 2) not all people and animals and plants are equal, and 3) the desert is a vast wasteland of inertness.

"But those are lies," say those who speak from Earth consciousness. Thus, for those who believe that we find truth in stories that narrate reconciliation between our inner and outer landscapes need to go back to a time before the history of patriarchal domination in order to hear one of those stories. This is precisely what Terry Tempest Williams did as she storied the experience of her family that lived downwind from the atomic radiation fallout in the state of Utah.

Linda Hogan takes the notion of *inner* and *outer* and pivots it to display another facet of meaning in an anthology she co-edited called *The Stories We Hold Secret: Tales of Women's Spiritual Development*. She agrees that reconciliation of *inner* and *outer* is important to both women and men; to women in particular, she finds that the reconciliation is the "courageous facing of our inner reality and outer facts." "Outer facts" are the lies told to women that have "harmed us and kept us down." Hogan says that we will no longer be kept down. "We tell on those who hurt us. We give away the truths of oppression. . . . We are the betrayers of the lie" and the lie is "the world's view of what is real" or "the facts."

"World" to Linda Hogan is that which goes against what our self's core, our Self, our center, our inner voices tell us is truth.

And, says Hogan, we are finally listening and gaining valuation in reclaiming our knowledge that "intuition, instinct, and life energy [are] our gifts" even though today, they are still judged as "gifts inferior."

The stories in the anthology are stories of women for whom the spiritual in everyday life, "is the waking and transforming, that is filled with growth . . . that is wise and healing." They are stories by women about women attempting "to come into right relationship with [their] world." Hogan writes that in reading the stories she received for the anthology, she felt reminded that "Growth comes from removing and removing, ceasing, undoing . . . fall[ing] into the core of our living Being." What does our Being tell us?: "Earth consciousness is the foundation of women's growing."[66]

Another writer concerned with telling the truth is Sally Carrighar in her narrative/memoir *Home to the Wilderness*. In writing this narrative, she accepted the challenge of an English critic to write "from the deepest level and withholding nothing." To Carrighar, "withholding nothing" required "an attempt to reach absolute honesty and that effort itself pushes one's consciousness down to a lower level." She then became determined to write her own truth. Sally Carrighar sees her story as "a dive, a descent" where she would find "a message from the very deep level of the subconscious." She felt filled with terror in the descent, and she recorded the terror. But she reached the level that brought as its reward, "loss of a degree of loneliness [and] a sense of coming back to a world where other people are more accessible."[67]

When she began the descent into herself to find truth, she did not know all the details that would go into her story. With this admission, she introduces readers to another facet of storytelling: all storytellers do not necessarily know the end of their stories when they begin them. Thus, all stories that are truth-bearing do not necessarily have beginnings, middles, and ends. Some, like Carrighar's, even begin in the middle.

Sally Carrighar's truth integrates her inner landscape with the outer landscape of her living by telling the truth about *her* life. She speaks with honesty, not hypocrisy; she creates an atmosphere where truth "became discernible as a pattern" and her story carries with it the power to heal a split in her that existed from the moment of her birth. The terror in her story is that her mother tried to kill her on several occasions as well as tried to live her life as if her daughter did not exist. So from the moment she was born, Sally was a cipher to her mother.

"What happened?" Sally Carrighar sustained nerve damage from her birth and her mother sustained what Carrighar's psychiatrist would call a "tear in the psyche." Carrighar's mother believed from the moment of birth that her daughter was a danger to her very existence and spent Carrighar's childhood and adolescent years trying to eliminate her. That truth was Sally's truth; it was not her father's or her brother's. Neither of them had even an understanding of the threat of their daughter's/sister's life that was taking place. And neither did Carrighar until she underwent two years of psychoanalysis with Dr. Carl Renz and Dr. Susanna Isaacs. She had put her bad experiences into her memory and then closed them off.

Though she did not enter therapy until she was out of college and had been working for some years, she was learning lessons about truth in her job as a "script girl" who assisted writers and workers in Hollywood in movie-making. There was an incident on a set one day: a lion broke away from his trainer and jumped from the set into the middle of the workers, settling in at Carrighar's feet. She had a brief vision of him as king, as free, as bounding across the grasses in his own country, and he had picked up on her vision. As they gazed at each other, trancelike, "a blaze of light stream[ed] into my mind: . . . I saw nature's truth, much more overpowering than even the clearest of human truth. From the lion's eyes . . . his truth was mine, too. Briefly ours was the Africa where bees hum, ants sing, and the hoofs of wild animals muddy water holes. . . . In this Africa of the animals, no mind ever deluded itself with romance, none ever milked any situations for others or for oneself."[68]

This incident causes her to quit her job even before the picture is finished, because "What I had thought of as human truth had always made it disturbing to live in the false atmosphere of Hollywood, but the glimpses of nature's much deeper truth had made it impossible to stay."[69] This insight gave me another thread to weave into the warp of storytelling: there is more than one truth.

"Human truth" and "nature's truth" can be the same, however, as I noted in Carol Snow's poem and in Paula Gunn Allen's description of pre-Conquest truth, and as I discovered in Barry Lopez's detailed description of landscape. They can also be put in opposition to one another, as they were in order to form the patriarchy. Such opposition has caused this culture to be vulnerable to a collective fragmentation, a collective tear in the psyche, if you will. A fragmented culture is a culture that is profane, not whole and is in need of healing. Tillie Olsen makes a similar observation to Sally Carrighar's when she writes about the unnatural silences that do not allow women to create, in particular: "the ignoring of societal roots, their causes, effects . . . the distortion of memory . . . all . . . diminish, make shallow, *falsify* [emphasis mine] one's writing."[70]

Jeanne Achterberg concurs when she points out that "when spirit no longer is seen to abide in matter, the reverence for what is physical departs."[71] Achterberg traces much of this social issue to the "Scientific Revolution when mind and matter were disjoined and spirit was conceptually eliminated from matter." Through the strategy of redefinition, "men could tear at nature (imaged as female) with mechanical devices" all in the name of the "new science." Another facet of truth, then, is *recognition* of this fragmentation. Two of those moments that are major for my understanding of what happens when human truth and nature's truth are fragmented and when one of the fragments dominates at the expense of the other fragments are: 1) the intrusion of the Pilgrims into the land and the spirituality of the people indigenous to what we now call the United States; and 2) the invasion of Christianity into the land and spirituality of the pagans who were Earth and goddess-conscious people.

The fragmentation occurred because the patriarchy brought with it dominance, an ideology of dialectic, a hierarchy, and a divorce between matter and spirit. These were elements that opposed a sustaining, connecting, patient, cyclic understanding of life, elements that were identified with goddess consciousness and with Earth as a dynamic—not something static or inert.

The patriarchy dominated through force, killing those who did not accept their beliefs, would not join their religion. Since those who represented the patriarchy exhibited a *tear in their psyches*, killing, plundering and conquering that which they thought threatened to destroy them, this meant killing those who held knowledge and wisdom of the universe in their role as crone, shaman, healer, or midwife.

Having linked women to nature and nature to Earth, plundering and conquering Earth was not far off. Neither was the desire to eliminate women and others ranked inferior in a patriarchal hierarchy. This desire drove the witch hunts of the fourteenth through the seventeenth-centuries where those patriarchs in power killed about eight million women . . . "and a few men." This desire drove those in power to use "he" as generic when talking of both male and female, thus excluding "she" from the context of knowledge for centuries. This desire drove Hitler to attempt to eliminate a race of people that he equated with evil. This desire drove the United States government to use the Western desert as a place to explode hundreds of atomic bombs in the '50s and '60s and '70s because the people, animals and vegetation that lived there were not considered important.[72] This notion of coupling female with nature and (white) male with power-over and dominance in society still drives the actions of our western culture, and we are still paying the price for that reversal.

In a speech called "Sex, Class and Race Intersections/Visions of Women of Color," Carol Lee Sanchez, sister to Paula Gunn Allen, tells her audience that "your 'civilization' has made us all very sick and has made our mother earth sick and out of balance. . . . You are the foreigners as long as you continue to believe in the progress that destroys our Mother." Audrey Shenandoah, Onondaga Clan Mother, addressed the Global Forum on Environment and Development for Survival in Moscow in January 1990. In her speech she told her audience:

> There is no word for "nature" in my language. Nature, in English, seems to refer to that which is separate from human beings. It is a distinction we don't recognize. The closest words to the idea of "nature" translate to refer to things which support life. . . . How can one be superior to that upon which one depends for life. . . . I would urge the whole concept of nature be rethought. Nature, the land, must not mean money; it must designate life. Western society needs to prioritize life-supporting systems and to quiet its commitment to materialism.[73]

Each of us, men and women alike, has scars from the cosmic fragmentation that occurred when the patriarchy came into history because we *are* Earth and are *from* Earth. No matter which other truths I know about myself, this one is the most basic. This is what I interpret Barry Lopez to mean when he emphasizes that we tell the truth in stories that integrate the exterior landscape and our inner landscape: the fusion of the human heart and the land. Body, mind and spirit should never have been separated, but in historical time, they were/are.

Each of the seekers after the truth that I write about in Part II at some time come to realize that they and Earth are one, that they contain properties of Earth, literally and metaphorically. Literally the water that housed each of us in our mother's womb contains the properties of the sea; in our veins, "a salty stream" in which the elements are combined in almost the same proportions as sea water"; our bones, "a heritage from the calcium rich ocean of Cambrian time."[74] At a point in our development, our human embryo cannot be distinguished from a chick embryo; we develop gills; we even develop tails before we evolve into human form and are born.

To discover "the truth" of Barry Lopez or "nature's deeper truth" of Sally Carrighar and to put it into story is to discover that we carry with us a symbiotic relationship to the land that bore us. No wonder the people who feed our dominant culture carry with them such a strong denial of aging and death: to acknowledge Earth and its cyclic characteristics that link us all to the female as well as to the birth/life/death cycle means losing not only corporate power but most importantly economic power. How can we make a profit if we stop tearing up and at the land with our mechanical devices in the name of progress and development? If, as a nation, we collectively acknowledged that truth, we would then need to take the next step and acknowledge the importance of women as co-creators. "In the beginning was thought, and her name was Woman. . . . She is the Old Woman Spider who weaves us together in a fabric of interconnection. She is the Eldest God, the one who Remembers and Re-members."[75] She is *Rio Abajo Rio*, the river beneath the river; *Luz del abyss*, the light from the abyss; *La Loba*, the wolf woman.[76] This western, industrial, technologized world is not ready for that step yet.

The cosmic split in her own life showed Sally Carrighar the need to write *her* own truth. Here, then, is another fact to *the truth*: We need not wait for the historical split that severed our ties to the Earth/universe to heal. We can heal the tear in us, individually. And because we are of earth/ Earth, each of us a strand in the web of life, healing our split, our strand will be a contribution to healing the cosmic split. We heal that split by finding our truth. As

I mend the break in my strand that connects me to life's web, I will contribute to healing the cosmic split. That split, that tear, that fragmentation is healed, mended, made whole by each of us finding our truth, our balance, our Beautyway.

Part III

"Tell me a story that's true"

Carol Christ wrote in 1980: "without stories there is no articulation of experience. . . . As people grow up, reach plateaus, or face crises, they often turn to stories to show them how to take the next step." This is especially important for women who "often live out inauthentic stories provided by a culture they did not create . . . [thus] women's stories have not been told."[1]

What has happened in the span of the years between 1980 and today has made a huge difference in women's stories getting told. Not only do we have women's stories in a generic sense, we now have Native American women's stories, African-American women's stories, lesbian stories, lesbian women-of- color's stories, Chicana stories, slave women's stories; the list goes on.

The texts in this section are some women's stories that cross generations, stories of women who reach plateaus and face crises. The stories and their writers are *Cactus Thorn* by Mary Austin, *The Dollmaker* by Harriette Arnow, *The Fires of Bride* by Ellen Galford, and *Send My Roots Rain* by Ibis Gómez-Vega. The women characters in these stories voice a need to find something. For some, the need is voiced early in the story; for some it is voiced later. However, for all of them, at one point, they are looking for the Self that connects them to their Earth-home. What they are looking for is unique in its particularity and common in its universality. I say "common in its universality," because *whether we know it or not,* we all have a connection to Earth, or, if we have lost that connection, a need to find it again.

The paths of these women's journeys do not follow a generic pattern. In their search for their truths and their identity, some of the women leave their homes and move to other regions; some do not. Leaving home is not a prerequisite for finding their truths. Some of them are more eager to take their journeys than others; some go on short journeys, some on long, and the paths are not straight.

Sally Carrighar reflected that we can never make up a good song (story) in order to please another person. "We make up songs as a way of saying something to others, something which already exists, and it is just waiting to be told." The women writers who created the women characters whom I have chosen to work with are "saying something" to me when I read their stories.

As I write what I perceive as the truths of these women writers and characters, I am telling my story as well: "something which already exists," something not told "in order to please another person," but "is just waiting to be told": the story that Nicole Brossard exhorts each woman to tell "at least once in her life."

My rooting of self to Self (and the need to root) came to consciousness when I gave birth to my first-born, Jason. It was the ancestral bonding between mother and child, the experience and its power that rooted me. The birthing not only bonded me to this new human that I had co-created, the process—birthing, and product—child—told me that he was from Earth. He was the part of me that cycled with the moon, that same moon that ruled the tides and produced Maria Milleny's seaweed woman (from *The Fires of Bride*). He was the part of me that loved to dig up the potatoes in the summer, the same potatoes that Gertie dug up to feel calm and rooted in Kentucky (from *The Dollmaker*). He was the part of me who, like Carole, wondered why her father would want to keep his childhood, his ancestry, hidden from her in a deadened silence, closing any and all doors to understanding those paternal roots (from *Send My Roots Rain*). He was the part of me that understood why Dulcie (from *Cactus Thorn*) committed a socially violent act in order to right and protect her relationship with Earth, because after Jason was born, I would have done anything that I had to do to protect him.

Once he was born, I no longer had the nightmare, recurring for years and years, that a man, hooded, dressed in black, constantly chased me in order to do me harm. The man never caught me, but I would awaken each time, heart throbbing, just seconds before he would catch me, having trapped me each time into a corner of a building. After Jason's birth, I no longer had that nightmare, because after Jason's birth, I no longer denied the female part of me. The bonding with Jason returned me to my Earth roots.

My second and last child Owen, helped me to grow those roots deep and strong. When he was three years of age, he taught me how to read the story of the universe in rocks; he taught me to remember and recall that all living things are connected as we walked the rocky beach of Lake Ontario looking for those elements under our feet that were telling us stories of the universe: of what used to be and what is now.

He taught me how to listen to what the trees were telling me. "I don't understand what they say, Owen." "You aren't listening in their language, Mom. They are talking to you. Right now they are talking."

Though my roots were now growing and deepening into the Earth of my Self, it was an act of the world that unsilenced me, helped me find my voice, an act that told me that the good girl could no longer be the silent girl. It was the day Owen was deliberately shot by a neighbor boy. The boy was eleven, Owen was nine. It was March 1990.

At the expense of my voice, I had been the good girl in the 1940s; at the expense of my sexuality, I had been the good teacher in the '60s and '70s; at the expense of personal growth, the good mother in the '80s. And my 'goodness' was not enough to keep the world running on track. (If I am good, I will not be hit and life will run smoothly.) Having my younger son shot was a violent way to teach me that silence is not golden, that many "if-then" propositions work only on paper, and that, though my life appeared to be harmonious and happy, inside, my Self was dying from not being fed because, like Arnow's Mrs. Anderson, I had become Tillie Olsen's essential angel. Granny in "Magic in a World of Magic" told the narrator that the soul can go only hours without nourishment. I had gone years.

It was in May of 1990 that I first heard of the Union Institute, the non-traditional university where I would eventually enroll in and finish a Ph.D. program. In October 1990, I made the entry colloquium. Looking back, my precipitous choice to apply, then accept Union's offer to enter their Institute came because of Owen's experience. Yet my voice had been trying to be heard for decades and decades. It is not that it was not speaking; rather, I had kept it silent, muted, masked. I had forced it to learn its "place." I denied it its own space from which to be heard. Unconsciously, I had learned my childhood lessons well, for I thought that because I was an independent person in many ways, I had a voice already. Not so.

And yet, like the water that floods towns, it was its own Self searching for space, for growth and a way to nourish that growth. To break out of the barriers I had imposed on it, it had to be released by an act of violence, because asking for release politely and quietly did not work.

I could have silenced that voice again, but I chose not to. My story of how I heeded the call of my voice to allow it to be heard through writing this book explains the choices I made to seek out primarily women's stories. I read and listened to many stories, long and short.

The four stories in Part II revealed more insights for me and my life than I had anticipated. Mary Austin's Dulcie, a woman Austin describes as being from the earth/Earth, is also analogous to the part of the flower for which the narrative is named: the cactus thorn. As the fragile and colorful essence of the cactus flower is protected from predators by a very sharp thorn, so too does Dulcie protect her fragile and colorful person with a knife that she carries with her at all times. So when Grant Arliss uses his power as the young patriarch to steal Dulcie's Being from her, she feels no guilt when she uses her knife to protect that Being. I have placed Dulcie's story first because, like Dulcie, I needed to "kill off" some of the denigrating and negatively authoritarian aspects of my life that were trying to rob me of my Self-connectedness before I could, like Dulcie, reroot and heal.

Harriette Arnow's Gertie, in Kentucky, is me when I was younger. I loved my contacts with earth and Earth. Like Gertie, I, too, left those contacts, but for different reasons. Gertie was forced to leave. I left so that the particular culture I lived in would not swallow me up like dead people are swallowed up when they are buried six feet under ground. Planting cut pieces of potatoes, knowing that they would transform into whole potatoes was one thing. Swallowed forever was another. Gertie's uprootedness from her birthplace was forced. Mine was by choice—to follow a larger goal: escape being swallowed up by the pre-feminist culture and community of the '40s and '50s where I was condemned to Hell for all eternity because I was born female.

Ellen Galford's Maria Melleny is a woman of the '80s who reaps the rewards of the sacrifices and risks made by countless women in the previous decades to pave a smoother path for women like herself. Although the history of women's roles was different for Maria than it was for me, she still had an uprootedness to her that nagged to be examined. As Maria journeys into the cratered night of female memory, I follow her easily. I understand that journey. When Maria roots to Earth and finds her Self, it is because she learns that the seaweed woman and the tenth-century nun were not only real, they were *her*. With that realization, Maria's artwork changes both in style and in quality. She knows what she has to do. She follows her Self that leads to her creative sculptures relating to her ancestors: the images of the goddesses, particularly the Celtic triple goddess, Bride. However, she has to return to her mother's ancestral roots on the island of Calleach in order to make that discovery.

Another reason I like Galford's characters and story is because of her perspective on Bride as Mary's midwife at the Nativity. After birthing Jason I realized there was more to the Nativity story than was reported in the Gospels. Something was missing; that "something" was the fullness of the Nativity experience: a midwife, labor, the birth, the first moment of contact between mother and child, the disposing of the afterbirth (did one of the animals in the stable eat it?), the cleaning up. Galford fills in the gaps missing from the Gospels.

Just as the Gospels are not to be taken literally, neither is Galford's interpretation. However, I had never read a revisionist perspective of the Nativity, and I find her interpretation as plausible as others find the interpretation in the Gospels.

Ibis Gómez-Vega's Carole needs to find her father's roots. When I began researching the questions that I wanted answered, I made conscious efforts to ask my mother and my brother direct questions about my deceased father's Irish heritage. My mother remembered nothing about his family, even when I insisted that she must, while she remembered details of her family that are amazing. My brother, who also wants to know more, remembers some things, and so we pool our information to piece this paternal patchwork past together. There is so much that will be lost forever. But I am now open to wanting to learn of that past that has been too painful for me to explore until now.

Like Carole and the other women in this story discover, that past, until recently hidden in darkness and silence, is not something to fear. My father could not speak of *his* past because it was too painful for *him*, and he died never having answered the call of his voice. Like Carole, as she moves through her story, I no longer need literal details. Using paternal memory as metaphor gives me power, insight, and understanding, as does reading stories like Carole's about searching her paternal ancestry and Maria's, about being rooted in an Irish/Celtic heritage.

Through these fictive women, I can see myself and, in reading their stories that are true, find comfort that I was not alone in my childhood experiences that were centered in silence and pain. Through these fictive women I can see that I am not alone in searching out an ongoing need to root self to Self, a need that I believe changes as the cycles of our lives change, and is ongoing in us for as long as we live.

Dulcie Adelaid: a woman from the Earth in Cactus Thorn
by Mary Austin

Mary Austin (1868–1934) lived in desert country for about thirty years before she wrote *Cactus Thorn* in 1927. When she was young, she and her family moved from a small town in Illinois to settle in the West. That move changed Austin's way of living and thinking. In the desert of the West, her favorite place to be, she learned to reject the "capitulation of young ladihood [sic]." The desert gave her the "courage to sheer off what is not worthwhile." The desert revealed to Austin "the bare core of things": the core of a person, of the environment, of life itself. She writes in her autobiography *Earth Horizon* that she sought "the Earth Horizon . . . the incalculable blue ring of sky meeting earth which is the source of experience. . . . The nurture of the spiritual life."[2] It is an image she borrowed from the Zia Indians and an image that guided the "bare core" of her writing, particularly in the last decade of her life, 1924–1934. She found that when one lived in the desert and came to love it, one was unable to be untrue to her or his core. Merely living in the desert is not enough; loving the desert, being receptive to its teachings is necessary if one is to discover one's own "bare core."

 She would tell people that three elements shaped the bulk of her art: Native American women artists, desert storytellers, and landscape. These three elements led to a proliferation of writing from 1903 until her death in 1934. *Cactus Thorn* is one of those writings. Written in 1927, it was not published until 1988 when Melody Graulich unearthed it from The Huntington Library archives. It was not published previously (and Austin was a well-known American writer in 1927) because publishers found it too radical. Apparently a distance in time now allowed the public of the 1980s to accept what was too radical in 1927.[3]

What was "too radical" is the fact that the female character, Dulcie, kills the male character, Grant Arliss, and goes unpunished for the deed. Mary Austin herself was driven by a need to put into story her version of her aborted affair with the well-known New York reformer, Lincoln Steffens. In Betty Lambert's novel *Crossings*, one of Lambert's characters says, "I want revenge. I'll get that bastard. I'll put him in a novel."[4] I was reminded of Mary Austin's comments on Lincoln Steffens when I read that quote. According to Austin, Steffens dumped her for another woman. Legally she could not kill him, so, indeed, to get revenge, Austin put Steffens in the novel as a character and killed him off. This character is a young man full of his own importance who is being groomed by the Eastern elite to become a senator from New York. He allows no one to stand in his way of success, fame, and fortune, even a woman he came to love in the desert southwest.

Austin wrote out her anger, and what she saw as her truth, in *Cactus Thorn*; being a skilled writer, she knew how to control that anger in order to draw the reader into her story of the desert and its influence, as well as her creative development of the desert and her two main human characters.

It is a story about the relationship between Grant Arliss, a promising politician from New York and Dulcie Adelaid, a young woman raised in the desert of the Southwest. It is also a story about "the power dynamics between women and men [that] transcends generations."[5] It is a story that is a striking example of what Elizabeth Minnich calls:

> paying very serious attention to phenomena long 'explained' as "natural," especially one of the most obvious and all-permeating facts of almost every society, the mutually implicated construction of sex and gender that gives men power over themselves and over women that women do not have. Gender becomes a subject

matter, a key to significations otherwise locked, a primary critical and revelatory tool of resistance and re-creation.[6]

Thus it is not only a personal story of the intimate life of a man and
a woman, it is also a story of cultural abuse acted out through the
misuse of power wrongfully perceived by a certain group of wealthy
men as the right to take and use whatever gets them to the goals
they have set for themselves, with no thought of the consequences
to the *other*.

The story opens with Grant Arliss on a train station platform
in the Southwest where he glimpses a young woman who seems to
him to blend into the landscape: "he could scarcely take her in,
lovely as she was, as a separate item of the landscape."[7] Arliss has
been traveling across the desert for two days, which was enough
time to be taken in by the "somnolent desert charm" (3), the charm
that "held him to the contemplation of the land's empty reach, its
disordered horizons, its vast, sucking stillness." (3)

To Arliss, this young woman "might, like the horned lizard
starting from under his feet, have assembled herself from the
tawny earth and the hot sand," (4). Through the narrative voice
that, for the moment, hides behind the eyes of Grant Arliss, readers
are introduced to a woman who may have been born from—risen
up from—the very earth and sand she sat on. We learn through the
narration that Grant Arliss has come to the Southwest to find himself and rid himself of a spiritual lethargy that has overtaken him.

In the opening pages of *Cactus Thorn*, readers learn that the
desert has an empty reach and sucking stillness, that the desert can
produce a human from its tawny earth and hot sand, and that the
desert is a place some people travel to, to find their lost Self. Arliss
is not the first to try to find himself in the desert, the woman born
from the earth tells him.

What Georgia O'Keeffe did with oils and brush, Mary Austin
does with words: she paints the desert in the multifaceted form

that magnetized and held people's attention. Through her narrator we learn about that magnetism: "Arliss could just make it out, a scar on the furthest range where the crude reds and ochers of the plain altered subtly to pearl and amethyst, and the rusty shadows began to creep from under the heavy glare, and fill the passes with blue drift." (6) With words instead of oils, Austin draws the reader into the story through Arliss's eyes—a New Yorker looking at earth's horizon with the aid of the woman from the earth, whom he refers to in his mind as "this girl." (4)

It is this same young woman who lets Arliss know that she knows where he is from, who like some "delicate insect, . . . took a sudden color of aloofness from the soil." (6) In order to regain control at being caught unaware by a stranger knowing anything about him, he puts her in the position of an insect. Unlike a real insect, however, he cannot stamp her out. And he *is* caught because he is out in the heat of the desert day, at a railroad junction waiting for his train that is late. His only physical escape is to pace, which he does, only to find that the woman has laid out an improvised table on bales of hay to serve lunch for two.

In the desert, evening begins to make its appearance shortly after lunch: "shadows begin to stir and crouch for their evening assault upon the plain, and the burnt reds and the thick yellows and pale ash of the desert clear and flash into translucent flame. In such moments one perceives the lure of the desert to be the secret lure of fire, to which in rare moments men have given themselves as to a goddess." (8)

Arliss equates Dulcie with this flame by observing how it "leaped subtly almost to the surfaces of this pale brown girl, as if she were, like the land." (8) Not on first reading, but on subsequent readings, readers gain a glimmer that this girl, Dulcie, *is* "the lure of the desert . . . the secret lure of fire." She also represents a goddess to whom Arliss will give himself. The giving will be unintentional, because Arliss is not a giver; he is a taker. The giving, however, will be his last Earthly act.

So caught up—and caught—by the unexpected qualities of the desert and the "girl," as Arliss insists on mentally calling this young woman, he wounds his fingers on the thorn of a cactus flower while collecting twigs to start a fire for tea water. The next incident turns into a foreshadowing, unknown to anyone, including the characters, until the end. But on re-readings, we see the sophistication in Austin's style as she plans this foreshadowing, using irony and an attitude of casualness in Dulcie's words.

> "There's only one way to admire a cactus," she commiserated, and while he fumbled for his handkerchief to swathe his pricked fingers, she held up the delicate blossom on the point of a dagger that she had produced unobtrusively from somewhere about her person. "I didn't know that the thorns simply jumped at you like that," Arliss apologized, taking the proffered dagger, not so much to admire the sun-rayed flower as to wonder at the implement on which it was impaled. It was slender like a thorn and had a carved ivory handle which had been broken and mended deftly with bone. He wondered where she carried it and what provocation would have brought it leaping against himself. (9)

Before the story ends, Arliss's curiosity will be satisfied on both accounts.

A new image enters the painting of the desert: desert-as-wounder. "The girl" defends this image by telling Arliss that 'The Desert's got a worse name than it deserves.'" (10) This "girl" knows the desert well; it may have a worse name than it deserves, but it is not all gentle and kind. Its nature is more expansive as well as more complex than that. The "girl" even admits that "the desert sort of sucks you up and throws you away." (10) But that does not make it evil, as Arliss implies. It throws you away "... *unless* you are willing to take what it gives you in place of what you had." (10) Arliss will pretend to do that, but in reality he never will, and that inability will be his undoing.

Arliss is not prepared for this "lure of the desert." He comes to
the desert to remove himself from the political scene of New York
that stole his energy; he comes to the desert an enervated man.
Therefore, he does not want to give up any more of himself to anyone or anything. He expects the desert to renew his vitality by
drawing energy from the desert. Feeling that the desert could take
the last of his waning energy frightens him.

If we equate "desert" with "nature," then nature is neither
good nor bad; however, it does have rules and *its* rules are more
powerful than *human* rules: ". . . unless you are willing. . . ." Indeed
Arliss is on to something when the early evening sky treats him to a
rare moment when he realizes in a flash of insight that, in certain
times, the desert's power carries the will of men to "give themselves as to a goddess." Arliss will be one of those men, and he will
die in sacrifice not even knowing that he dies giving himself as to a
goddess in order to right an imbalance that he had manufactured.

The desert/nature decides what will be the interchange with
those who come to it: "It's [the reason to come to the desert] taken
out of your hands and unraveled; all you have to do is watch it
being set right . . . [the desert] teaches you never to make anything
up." (10, 11)

In chapter 1, then, we meet the "girl" who, as yet, had no
name but who comes out of the desert, the earth; we meet Grant
Arliss, a gentleman from New York City who has a need to renew
his sagging and lethargic spirit by encountering the desert; and we
meet the desert itself, from whom the young woman has "grown"
and learned its rules.

At the opening of chapter 2, Mary Austin uses Grant Arliss to
tell the readers that in *his* eyes, he is a morally upright politician.
His voice, he feels, has been "the only voice of hope and faith"
raised among the post-World War I generation of politicians. He
has been inspirational only because he can appeal to any group to
whom he spoke; he can appeal to any group because he is aligned

with none of them: "He had been neither Anarchist, Communist, Socialist, Syndicalist, nor an adherent of any of the codified sociological situations." (18) By not being aligned, by having no historical, political, or ethical opinions, he represents to the reader a man who considers neutrality an acceptable stance of the Social Reformer: "what America needed was pure politics based upon intelligent comprehension of her situation." (19)

Along with the aid of a powerful political leader in New York, and his unmarried daughter, Grant Arliss is on his way to being elected to a seat in the Senate. The election is all but secured when he flees west. He is wavering and doubtful about his ability to continue to be so pure in his stand, however, because the women he knew would not inspire him the way he needs inspiring by women. He needs them to give themselves to him willingly and selflessly, when called. He does not want to give himself over to the fire; the pull to do so frightens him. But he wants women to give themselves over to him. He believes that such is his right as a man, and such is the role of women. For him, indeed, as Minnich writes, "[g]ender becomes a subject matter, a key to significations otherwise locked. . . ."

Austin writes with strong, almost cynical irony here in characterizing Grant Arliss, using him sometimes as a narrator but obviously an unreliable one. On the one hand, she creates him as a sensitive, post-World War I male doing his best to revive the sagging morale of those Americans who participated "in a war as unacceptable as it proved inconclusive." (17–18). On the other hand, Austin reveals a man who thinks that "it was the business of women . . . to keep the fire burning [. . .] priestesses of the flame." (13) When he flees to the desert, he finds a girl who does not believe that women were the priestesses, but who believes that women "*lived* in the flame . . . like a fire in the depths of the earth, or a fire in the sun." (14, 13)

The young woman is not finished giving her opinion about why Arliss feels the way he does about women when she tells him, as she shakes off the crumbs from the tablecloth that held their noon meal: "that's one of the ways in which women got sidetracked. They didn't *have* to keep making up the fire all the time, the way men do. They *lived* in the flame until men got to thinking of them as being makers of the flame."(14)

In Arliss's flight from his city community to what he had hoped would be a place where his rules would be abided by, he finds just the opposite. He finds a female who will not fan his fires; instead she is, to him, "Almost as stinging as the cactus thorn." (20) She is the lure of the desert, the fire. Arliss is pulled to her against his will, as some men have been pulled to the desert.

Austin begins to build in the reader a tension of polarities whereby the man trying to control the poles, loses control because of the female and the desert: the desert he flees to, to regain control, and the female who will not share his definition of "the business of woman." The downward spiral begins as Arliss fights to maintain a balance in his life through control. As Austin paints him, for Arliss to lose control is tantamount to losing his Self, the inner person, the "bare core" that is what he is, or at least what he thinks he is.

Even his friend Fernald shares his view of women. It is when Fernald tells Arliss that the West is "a great country. . . . And a man-size job to conquer her . . . [sic] make her bear . . . [sic] great civilizations" (24) that Arliss receives the impetus he needs to flee to the desert: to prove his manhood through conquering the land; to find a woman to kindle a flame and keep it going; to find great (read "passive") country. Arliss heads for the great country, more specifically a deserted villa.

Arliss, a man uprooted from his inner identity, does not know what has caused that uprootedness, that sense of ennui. Though the girl has told him how to find wholeness of spirit again, (9) obviously he has neither listened nor believed her since he still is looking for "a lovely, sleepy women tend[ing] a little lipping flame." (27)

As the sun is setting on the first day in the villa, Arliss realizes that he has a companion: the young woman. When he comes upon her, it is as the sun is setting. As she tells him why she is inhabiting the mansion, she stops in mid-explanation to point out the setting sun: "every hill . . . translucent with secret fire mounting suddenly out of the earth's core." (33) In the next passage, the "it" is the background of desert at sunset that Austin brings to life when the woman whispers: "It is thinking of the time when it was all molten with the earth's fire . . . by and by it will begin to think of the time when it was blue with the sea from which it rose. . . . They say the sea came in there [at the foot of a range] not so very long ago. Times like this it comes back." (33)

The young woman not only knows the primordial history and the cyclic pattern of the desert, she accepts these as a truth. Because she accepts the desert's laws/realities, she can be seen as "assembled from the tawny earth." She not only knows that to try to dominate and conquer the desert is impossible, but she knows that the desert makes the rules. She knows how to take what the desert gives; to do that, she empties her mundane self so that the spiritual Self can be receptive to what the desert has to give.

It is only after their shared moment with the sun setting and the history of the earth momentarily touching their souls that Arliss —and the readers— finally learn the name of the girl: Dulcie Adelaid Vallodon. "Vallodon" is her mother's name; her father's, "Kennedy." So we have a young woman who is in her early twenties—"girl" to Arliss, identified as "woman" by the mediating narrator—voluntarily assuming her mother's name after her mother's death, as a way to remember the matrilineal side of her ancestry. Dulcie Adelaid is white; however, her mother reared her with the help of the nearby Indian women. Thus Dulcie's attitudes about living and about the desert, are tribal, not colonial.

The male character's name we learn in the opening sentence—in fact his name opens the story. He stands out from the scene as separate from his environment from the moment the mediating narrator introduces him in line one; Dulcie does not stand out as a separate being until a third of the way through the narrative, after their shared moment with the primordial transformation of the desert by the setting sun.

While Arliss lives in the mansion, he has a maid, an Amerindian woman, who delivers food, firewood and an orderly room daily; with such services, he begins to feel "accepted by the land, free to absorb himself into its wide spaces and healing stillness." (37) Acceptance and healing do not spring only from daily maid service; that is available to him in the East. Temporary release from inexorable domestic chores gives the *opportunity*, the time; however, Arliss then must use that opportunity to empty out the old, even dead thoughts that can lay hold of one's spirit the way cold and dampness can lay hold of one's bones during a long eastern winter. If he can let go of the thoughts that enchain him, and then wait for the healing effect of an emptied stillness, he will begin to feel acceptance by the land. That acceptance can begin a healing process.

Grant Arliss is not yet ready, however, for authentic acceptance. That he will never be ready is his ultimate tragedy. His need to control, to hold onto and dominate his thoughts, his inability to let go of the ennui from his eastern experiences overpower even his best intentions. The mediating narrator is preparing us for the ultimate moment of tragedy that comes at the very end.

This same narrator is also preparing us to realize that this story is not only about Arliss's inability to let go of his narrow-visioned philosophy of women, land and power, but that this is a story about the desert and a woman who learns that by living according to the ways of that desert, she remains an authentic and whole person. Arliss so dominates the first half of the narrative that Dulcie's character and attributes are gleaned only by reading between the lines and in back of the words. Arliss is foreground; Dulcie and the desert and the fire are background.

One tragic characteristic about Arliss is his lack of insight into his own double-standard view toward Earth and women. As a politician he has denounced strip mining the desert and the lack of child labor laws with the facility of "the born politician." (39) But when Dulcie begins an animated discussion with him in the villa about why he was so popular with women, he becomes annoyed with her for her lack of understanding of politics and economics. She then tells him:

> "You could say it about children," she insisted, "because women were listening to you. It's something women have been waiting for somebody to say. It's something they've always wanted known. About personal quality being an asset, I mean. That's what makes them suffer so when men mistreat them. It is because the thing in them that is injured is all they have to give."
> . . . Arliss frowned. He had been thinking of industrial despoiliation; he hadn't, any more than most men, comprehended that unification of woman's nature that leads her to see in every infringement an assault upon her femininity. He found it disappointing that this girl of the wilderness should exhibit the tendency that annoyed him so much in more sophisticated women, to "lead the subject back to sex," when it so clearly had to do only with economics. (40)

A feminist reader sees that it is not Dulcie who does not understand, it is Arliss. Three weeks in the desert has not even scraped the dust off of his tunneled view of women.

Dulcie, unaware of Arliss's inability to expand or transform his conventional and traditional notions on women, proceeds to explain to him, in one of the most important passages in the story concerning women and nature, just how she has learned to live as a wise woman, though young:

> "When I'm out with the Indian women . . . gathering roots and materials for basket making, it's not that I expect to make baskets or drink their medicines, it's the things you sort of soak up

from the earth while you're with them, the things that make
women wise . . . it's not as if they learned about willows and
grasses in order to make baskets, but as if they learned to make
baskets by knowing willows. I guess men used to learn that way
once—learned to make bows by knowing junipers the way their
branches bend and spring back. But now they try to do all their
learning in their heads." (41)

Dulcie wants Arliss to understand that both men and women
need to listen to the language of the willow and juniper in order to
succeed at living in the desert. The way one listens to that language
is not with ears and mind alone but also with the body, the spirit,
and what some call the inner ear. Arliss perceives Dulcie's activities
as "resorting to a primitiveness that was not the fierce, food-
snatching struggle of the cave men of fiction, but a surrender to
informing and creative intimacies with earth and fire and root and
stone." (41, 42) Arliss, however, continues to use his habitual way
of looking at the wilderness by choosing to think as a patriarchal
male: "struggle of the cave men" (42), a man-sized job to conquer
her (24), opposing the female who surrenders to "creative intimacies with earth . . ." (41) Dulcie does not do the dividing of tasks and
attitudes, because she recognizes that males can also understand
tree talk; it is Arliss who does the dividing: men struggle with
nature, women surrender to nature. Austin's irony reaches the
reader when she puts the narrator of the story inside Arliss's mind:
"And instantly with this lightning flash which she threw across the
nature of women, as closer always to the moulding realities of
earth, . . ." (42) Dulcie has done no such thing; Arliss leaps to the
conventional lie that women are closer to nature than men.

Though male and female once thought alike in Dulcie's sense
of history, she sees that males and females have separated on fundamental points; to Dulcie, when men and women began to use
"'made-up ideas'" (46) about marriage, society, religion and politics instead of allowing nature—in this case the desert—to "'go on
by itself, doing things that you don't see either the beginning of, or

the end'" (47), then we got into trouble. Arliss, however, thinks that if he can get to people, "teach them to think things out for themselves," (47) then the world will be a better place.

Dulcie's attitude is that it is the thinking that has gotten the world into trouble. Dulcie sees that the solution to troubles like marriage, strip mining, and child labor is to "keep still," and "the way would . . . come forth like a wild thing and show itself." (47) For Dulcie, "It" is our ultimate teacher of how to live. "It" is Tao-like in that we learn the path to living, wisdom and knowledge through listening with our whole being to what "It" is teaching us. She tries to explain to Arliss what the desert is able to do for him. He gets lost in one of the earlier chapters when he goes walking by himself. "You were just thinking and thinking, weren't you? And suddenly you were lost. That was because you got away from—It. . . . If you had waited, just held still and waited, It would have come back. You would have found yourself." (47)

Dulcie is not aware that Arliss still is unable to understand that the desert is not a place to fear, and so she continues with an analogy to city life. Dulcie does not cast aspersions on city life, but she does see that there are more people in the city who have "gone off by themselves and . . . were beginning to run around and shout to one another that this was the way, and this. But if they would keep still, the way would have come forth like a wild thing and shown itself." (47)

She feels that more destruction comes through what is "made up" by men, by shouting and running around, than through the desert that catches people unawares, "sucks you up empty and throws you away." (10) What goes on by itself is the apparent wild disorder of the desert: "It can use men. It *will* use them, but It can get on without them." (47)

This aspect of the desert, catching men unawares, almost gets Arliss killed early on because he takes a nap out on a rock in the sun of summer. A rattlesnake looking for mice near a water hole is ready to bite him when Dulcie, understanding the ways of a rattler, pins it quickly to the earth before it strikes Arliss. Dulcie, knowing that a rattler will not strike before giving off the death-rattle warning, strikes before the snake sounds its warning. Dulcie, knowing the way of the desert, keeps her city companion from being sucked up by the wild disorder of the desert. (47) To do so she uses the same dagger she has used to cut the thorn from the cactus flower, the thorn that wounded Arliss in the beginning of the story. Arliss sees the instrument as "a small dagger *like* a thorn" (50) [emphasis mine] So the dagger has now become the thorn that it, the dagger, once removed from the flower—with Dulcie's help.

It is this experience that advances their relationship from companions to lovers. As Dulcie performs an act that Arliss is grateful for, he then is placed in the position of surrendering himself to her, something that Arliss believes only women do—surrender themselves. Aware of the moment as one that is temporarily reversing the yin/yang order of his interpretation of his world-view, Arliss returns the order to how he views the "right" way of male/female relationships by sexually conquering (but not raping) Dulcie; the turning brings to fruition his new insight: "that that thing happened which he had supposed from the first must happen . . . she had become the woman of his desire." (51) Dulcie, herself caught in the chaos of the moment, does indeed surrender to his touch and his desire. (52)

Arliss succeeds, then, in righting the chaos that placed him in an uncomfortable position—loss of control over his life—as Austin links sex and death in a scene that will presage the future of both characters. Neither knows that the tables will turn and that Arliss will become the rattlesnake as Dulcie becomes the unsuspecting, momentary victim.

The opening to this future begins when, on one of their excursions to the foothills of the mountains, Dulcie reveals more of her view that the desert is to be surrendered to by both men and women; she asks Indian George, a long-time friend, to take Arliss deer hunting into the hills. Dulcie, however, will not go. When Arliss tries to goad her, she replies: "Haven't you ever seen anything that made you think that there is a different kind of rightness for different kinds of people? If I were to go against the wild things, something would happen to me." (56)

Arliss, predictably, thinks he understands by pointing to men he knows who are "the very fountainhead of economic corruption and yet die happy in their beds. . . ." (57) Dulcie's reply to that lays the foundation for her future actions: "It was because they didn't go against their Medicine, as the Indians say. . . . So long as we don't do anything to interfere with what is using us, anything to make ourselves unusable, I think It doesn't pay very much attention to us." (57)

Arliss thinks that Dulcie is being coy and cute when she talks about "Medicine" and "It": he asks her if it is all right for him to kill a deer and not be punished. Dulcie tells him yes, but if he goes against his Medicine, "to spread justice and honesty into business and trade and society" (57), then he will be punished. His only response to Dulcie's serious and reflective approach to life is to say, "You are a pagan, Dulcie, . . . and your gods are highly utilitarian." (57) Quick to respond to his desire to shake off an understanding that, as with the rattler incident, would take away his illusory control over his life, she says, "They've got to be, with the earth and all the worlds to attend to! Why should they bother about the little things we do for ourselves and each other so long as we don't get in their way? . . . I should be afraid to tell a lie or to kill a deer, but I am not afraid about us." (57)

Dulcie's gods—those of the earth and the other worlds—were set in motion a long, long time ago. We are but *a* part if "It," not *the* part. For Dulcie, doing no harm, not going against our inner selves, our personal integrity that defines each of us as who we are, our Medicine, is how we live our lives so as not to call down punishment.

What is interesting about Dulcie's use of the the word "pun-ishment" is that she does not define it. As readers, however, we know what she thinks is right—and wrong—for her, and for her and Arliss. What is right for her and Arliss is that she knows that "I wouldn't need to make up anything with you." (47) What is right for her, she tells Arliss, is to kill a man who is spoiling her chance at life: "making it so miserable I couldn't endure it—and there wasn't any other way of dealing with him—." (58)

Dulcie thinks that she and Arliss are "right" for each other—Medicine. Arliss thinks so, too, but only on the desert, not in New York City. Dulcie and New York. Well, that he would consider—later. Arliss's condescending attitude toward Dulcie and her quaint philosophy that is undergirded by relative morality and defined by personal integrity and consistency gives an opening to his fatal flaw. Melody Graulich writes that "Arliss's fatal flaw . . . is his unconscious hypocrisy, his shortsighted self-knowledge." (105) Elizabeth Flynn would call his fatal flaw, his inability to become part of what he had seen as "Other." Not becoming interactive with his "Other," but maintaining that dominating stance of detached distance that Elizabeth Minnich says "gives men power . . . over women that women do not have," he would go against his Medicine and bring on his own demise.

Even three months in the desert with Dulcie cannot shake him of his shortsighted need to control his life and others, so that political success will one day be his, won by his rules, not by his Medicine. He does not care for "the Intellectuals" (59) he must pander to in New York City to get elected, and yet he will go against his Medicine for that success in election. Considering Dulcie in New York City is not a thought that he wants to confront. Because Dulcie thinks that she and Arliss have a relationship that is not "made up," Dulcie does not think twice about *not* going with him: "Nor does he wish to leave her. The question is how to keep her "secret well of refreshment" in his active life. Arliss has learned nothing in these three months, particularly about women, and

nature, and "bare core." Although Dulcie is unaware, the disinte-
gration of their relationship begins.

Arliss's self-knowledge is so shortsighted that he lies to a
drunken man who comes to the villa looking for Dulcie by sending
this man during the season of unexpected sandstorms to a place
that has no water. "'You've made the desert seem so safe to me . . .'
he told her" (69), which is not the attitude that *Dulcie* conveys; it is
the attitude that Arliss wants to be *his* understanding of the desert.
Nobody who knows the desert is allowed to send anyone else out in
sandstorm season to a place with no water, no matter how
drunken, disagreeable, or unacceptable the person is. So Austin
sets the reader up for more Medicine transgressions on Arliss's
part. Three years in the desert will not change him, let alone three
months. He is selfish and power-hungry, and even his relationship
with Dulcie will not round his edges, will not give him these flashes
of insight he believes he is capable of receiving.

What he does not know is that the man he sends away is
Dulcie's husband, come to reclaim her. That Dulcie felt "exploited"
(74) by her husband, the drunken and disagreeable stranger, (he
had raped her after they were married), and has not felt exploited
by Arliss is not a flaw in her perception at this juncture. Her husband, in fact, has exploited her, and while in the desert, Arliss has
not. Of course not; he was not near his center of power, New York
City, so he could live in and for the moment with the heightened
awareness found when everyday pressures of one's ongoing roles in
life are lifted.

But ongoing "heightened awareness" is not to come to Arliss,
even in the moment where, as with the rattler, he and Dulcie are in
the presence of death: Dulcie's husband is dying in a cabin where
the three of them wait out a sand storm. Arliss is filled with pity and
sympathy for her as she tells him of the exploitation: ". . . the same
sort of sympathy he might have had for a young quail, hiding itself
timidly in the sand at his feet." (74) This man has not allowed the

desert to pass through him as a way to heal his spiritual lethargy; he is still caught in the cultural lies that tell him that women are lower than men—animals under foot, while he uses words with Dulcie to entice her to believe that they share an equal and "right" relationship. After all, he needs his well of refreshment, his flame. He has learned nothing from the desert that he came to learn, nor from the woman who represents the silence, aloofness, and wildness that is the desert, the element of the desert that can heal the person who wants to be healed. (10, 50)

When he returns to New York, his followers "found themselves dazzled into confidence. Dazzled and yet warmed. There was a blaze, a sensible heat." (79) Unknowingly, Dulcie has become the fanner of that blaze/flame as Arliss takes from her what he wants a woman to give him: "it was the business of women . . . to keep the fire burning." (13)

Not only does he not give himself over to the desert to erase his spiritual lethargy, he uses the one woman in his life who consciously despises being used by a man in the way Arliss uses her. As Arliss sits at dinner with his political sponsor and his sponsor's daughter, he consciously closes the door on Dulcie: "Already that episode was being blown over in his memory, buried . . . with the clean sand of relief." (81) His downfall is not far off as, once again, he goes against his Medicine, choosing to forget Dulcie, as Alida, his sponsor's daughter, sees to his material comforts: "the cozy fire, the shaded light, the choice but simple meals" (82); "daily maid service." (37) She is a flame fanner.

His rapid downfall comes when he refuses to acknowledge that Dulcie's appearance in New York City, three months after he left her in the desert with her drunken and dying husband, is because of him. The obtuseness of this man, coupled with his inability to be transformed by his desert experiences, cries out to the reader the depth and breadth of Arliss's societal power built upon the rules established by the patriarchy to charm and to move the intended audience for his own political and self-centered desires to be met. He does not care whether child labor laws are passed or democracy served; he cares that *he* is served, served by those people, places, and things put on this earth to serve him: money, voters, women, and nature.

Dulcie comes to New York to resume her "right" relationship with Arliss. When Dulcie tells Arliss that she is "not afraid about us" (57) because they feel right for each other, she places herself in an equal relationship with him, one where the Other was not an object, but both were subjects, coordinating in a conjunctive relationship. Arliss even assents to this—in the desert: where the regions are wild, untamed, he assents. Back in the city, where women are flame fanners, he does not assent. In other words, Arliss follows rules relative to his *place* of being, not to his *being*; Dulcie follows the rules of her *being*.

So when Dulcie relates to Arliss that she stayed with her husband until he died in order to give comfort to his dying, she reminds Arliss: "I realize that the only thing that saved me was the recollection of how we had always agreed together, you and I, about people not having the right to seek their own way at the expense of others." (86) Dulcie stayed to give comfort to her dying husband rather than go back to New York with Arliss so as not to make her husband—or Arliss—an object; Arliss left Dulcie in the desert precisely because she was not a "subject" to him but an "object." Spreading justice and honesty for Arliss does not extend to women, even the woman who shows him how to use the desert to be healed of his spiritual lethargy. He becomes politically successful while becoming spiritually corrupt.

The corruption takes a turn to hypocrisy. He gives a speech about "'the *rights* of people taking precedence over what we *feel* about them' and 'the only sound politics being an expression of the reality of human experience.'" (87) Speeches and words not backed by actions, he tells Dulcie of his marital engagement to Alida in a cafe that was "quiet without being too excluded." (89) Dulcie reacts

to the news of the engagement as one would expect—with hor-
ror—"as one arrested on the brink sees the abyss widening below."
(90)

Dulcie may live in the nearly uninhabited desert, the antithe-
sis of New York City, but she is no fool when it comes to understanding different types of people. As Arliss tries hard to cover the
choice to marry Alida, in the street outside the cafe—where
"scenes can lose some of their intensity," Dulcie cries out: "That
you should do such a thing like this! I'd *heard* of such things—
men who used all the forms of honor and high mindedness to get
what they all the time meant to throw away—." (92) This, in a nut-
shell, is exactly why Dulcie's final act toward Arliss is justified in
her eyes, when "all the time" he never meant to be open to the
desert, to be interactive with her. He is a man looking for creature
comforts to satisfy him. The object to satisfy? A woman. Since one
woman, particularly one who could be compared to a lizard or a
quail, is nowhere near worth what the daughter of a wealthy political sponsor is worth, Arliss thinks that he can indeed exploit Dulcie
to meet his needs.

Dulcie is not the daughter of a wealthy political sponsor; she is
the daughter of the desert, perhaps the desert itself in human form,
having "assembled herself from the tawny earth and hot sand." (4)
She knows her bare core; she knows her Medicine; she knows her
personal integrity, and she knows the rules that govern the
integrity of others—from the cactus flower to the rattlesnake to
Grant Arliss. Except for her husband who has been foisted upon her
by her father, she has never met anyone who goes against his or her
Medicine. If one wishes to live a compatible life in harmony with
the rest of the universe, one does not commit the act against others
that Grant Arliss commits against Dulcie. Arliss commits such an
act when he not only excludes Dulcie from his life, beginning with
the day he leaves the desert, but when he perfunctorily chooses
another woman to marry without telling the other woman about
Dulcie or Dulcie about the other woman.

Arliss would not agree to a meeting of the three of them, even though to Dulcie that was the only way "to untie the knot" (93) between Arliss and herself so that he and the other woman could be free to tie *their* knot. Dulcie decides not to fight for Arliss. She is willing to leave his life, but only after they untie their knot, the two threads that had entwined and bound them in their relationship. She would leave with no hard feelings.

So keen is Dulcie on being true to her Medicine—"I should be afraid to tell a lie or to kill a deer, but I am not afraid about us"(57)—that when she pushes for a meeting of the three, Arliss yells at her in the privacy of his apartment: "Don't you dare! You hussy—if I catch you, disturbing —anybody— I'll know how to deal with you!" (93) Yelling at her is painful enough, but for Arliss to label Dulcie as "hussy" is the ultimate act of Medicine treachery. In patriarchal language and point of view, "hussy" implies a woman who shamelessly uses her desire, dress, and actions to trap a man for her personal desires. In calling her "hussy" in his scornful way, Arliss steals Dulcie's soul, her Self; he empties her will.

According to Sandra Ingerman, one person steals the soul of another because "their survival depends on the other person's life force."[8] Such a theft summons up the image of a folkloric vampire, whose story is that it needs the blood of the living in order to continue to survive itself. Arliss's political and personal survival depends on him stealing the souls, the lifeblood, of women, sucking them up empty and throwing them away. (90)

There is only one way that Dulcie, being Dulcie, can react to her soul being stolen: "Dumb, hurt and anguished unbelief stared at him from her startled eyes . . . and with a low cry of animal pain she turned and ran from him with the stagger of a wounded wild creature toward its lair." (93)

When they meet for the last time, "he saw what had gone on in her; the wreck and damage of illimitable despair. . . . To his credit, he was incredibly touched by her appearance." (96) The ingratiation does not last long, however, because from his point of view, Dulcie becomes once again, a girl, this time, "Poor girl. . . ." (97) For a moment a sense of compassion flickers through Arliss's mind, but a moment is all that sense stays with him. Immediately he distances himself from her by murmuring "poor girl," when in the desert, she had become woman to him.

In his apartment, at their last meeting, Dulcie reminds Arliss what she has earlier narrated to him about her relationship with her husband while the two of them tended to this dying husband—a narration born of a two-year separation from the husband: "'But I couldn't feel, in spite of being married, that it was right for *him* to have me just—just for his pleasure. I felt— exploited,' she found the word finally. 'And before I met you, I knew that you didn't believe in the exploitation of women.'" (73–74) And now to Arliss she says: "So I wasn't real to you, ever . . . I was just used—exploited—in the eternal war—the war between men and women." (98) As he is hugging her to say goodbye, he is honestly shocked by "a sudden surprising pain in his side like a thorn." (98) Dulcie stabs Arliss to death with the knife she has used to cut the thorn from the cactus flower and to kill the rattlesnake: as the police described it, "a thorn-shaped dagger of foreign workmanship, the ivory handle mended with bone." (99)

The killing of Grant Arliss by Dulcie Adelaid is not a surprise to the reader who has been aware of the many foreshadowings. Previous to the killing, Austin compares Dulcie to the cactus flower that carries with it its own protection from harm, a thorn. Covered by the petals, in the middle of the flower is a thorn that is sharp enough to sting and draw blood when the flower is in danger. Looking back, then, we notice that Austin ever so subtly paints a likeness between Dulcie and the flower, her dagger and the thorn.

Austin also paints a likeness between Dulcie and the desert. The lure of the desert is the lure of Dulcie. The lure of fire is the lure of Dulcie. Arliss uses this likenesses when he is with Dulcie in the desert in their first days together. All through the development of their relationship in the desert, he makes allusion after allusion to Dulcie, either as emerging from that land or as like the land herself.

When Dulcie kills Arliss, she is following her Medicine because when she, like the desert and the cactus flower, is violated, something must be done to right the chaos that comes from the violation. Balance and harmony are fundamental laws of the desert.[9]

Therefore, killing Arliss with the knife she carries for her protection is the act that frees Dulcie of the pain caused by having her soul stolen, the act that heals the wounded wild creature, the woman, the flower, the desert. Symbolically, Dulcie is more than Dulcie; she is the land that has been wounded. Arliss has done the wounding, and a serious wounding it is, since he considers both Dulcie and the land an object to be conquered. (24)

Rather the reader agrees or disagrees with Dulcie's act (and one of my friends and I have had several conversations about that act), Austin uses that act as the catalyst for Dulcie to start her healing. Whatever the reader's opinion, Austin consistently set up Dulcie's act of killing Arliss as one that was healing. Thus, in 1927, indeed in a radical way, Austin tried to expose a lie concerning the construction of gender that would not be "heard" for half a century: that men do *not* have "power over themselves and over women that women do not have."[10]

Austin concludes her narrative with the following sentence:

> There was nothing known of Arliss or his life which could connect the weapon, "a thorn-shaped dagger of foreign workmanship, the ivory handle mended with bone," with the figure of a young woman who at the moment this decision was being arrived at was staring blindly at the fleeting of Western landscape past the windows of the Overland Flier, her face slowly setting into the torpor of relief after great shock and pain. (99)

Returning to the desert, to the place that taught her "never to make anything up" where she has learned to be "a part of the big pattern," (11) Dulcie could heal completely and continue to live in the flame of earth, soaking up from the Earth the things that make women wise.

The Journeys of Gertie and Mrs. Anderson in The Dollmaker by Harriette Arnow

Gertie in Kentucky

Gertie Kendrick Nevels is the main character in *The Dollmaker* by Harriette Arnow. She lives in the hill country of Kentucky on a rented farm with her husband Clovis and their five children: Cassie Marie, Amos, Clytie, Enoch, and Reuben. Her husband hates farming as much as Gertie loves it. Because Gertie does most of the work, both are satisfied with where they live and what they do.

As a woman of her Earth-home in Kentucky, a basic assumption that underlies Gertie's life is the wholeness and unity of the cosmos, and her relationship to all forms of life. This assumption makes Earth and the cosmos a sacred space; working the earth and talking with the stars and the moon and the trees keeps Gertie rooted, whole, and happy. In Kentucky, she lives her life according to the rituals of the farm that, by their nature, are tuned to the cycles of the seasons, the rising and setting of the sun and the moon. Farm cycles and nature's cycles work in conjunction with each other. In Kentucky, she does not own a clock; she does not need one when the sun, the shadows, the moon's cycles, and the seasons of the year tell her the time to milk, to plant, to reap.

She grows everything that the family eats: "the new hominy fried in lard. . . . It was good with the shuck beans, baked sweet potatoes. . . . Gertie served it up with pride, for everything, even the meal in the bread, was a product of her farming."[11] She even "grew" the pig, slaughtered with her own hands—that gave the lard. She prefers to be out of doors: "Mrs. Hull's house, like her mother's and

most houses, smothered her. It was good to be alone back in the
potato patch." (104) She measures time by the seasons: "A yellow
envelope like that had come for Jesse back in dogwood-blooming
time, and another for Henley (Gertie's brother) a little after
molasses-making time." (116) Those yellow envelopes brought
news of death from the war, and the remembrances of the deaths of
loved ones were tied to the cycles of the seasons. The cycles were
ways of remembering.

However, although she loves her children and the creative
aspects of mothering, and working the farm in its cycles and seasons, she has another kind of calling burning in her: the need to
carve and whittle with her special knife. She transforms pieces of
wood from the trees in her area into anything and everything—
dolls, beds, dressers, chairs, and handles, especially handles: "hoe
handles, saw handles, ax handles, corn-knife handles, broom han-
dles, plow handles, grubben-hoe handles, church-dasher handles,
hammer handles, all kinds of handles." (22) Her favorite piece of
wood is a piece of wild cherry wood in which she hopes to find the
right face to carve into it. The face of Christ intrigues her more
than any other face, but the face does not yet come through clearly
enough for her to begin the act of transformation. That nagging to
find the right face keeps Gertie's thoughts occupied when she is
not tending to children, her crops, her parent's crops, the chickens, and handles.

For Gertie, even the way in which she approaches the piece of
wood in her spare time is important: with awe and reverence, knife
in hand. In other words, Gertie approaches the wood in such a way
that shows she is aware that she and the wood share a symbiotic
relationship to the cosmos. The cosmic relationship in Gertie's
vision is the interaction she initiates between the block of cherry
wood, once a tree on her father's land, and a face that she knows is
in that wood, just waiting to be brought forth.

Harriette Arnow describes and forms the character of Gertie
in such a way that, to me, she is quintessential Earth Woman; she

is as large in vision as is the story that Arnow creates, a story that more accurately can be called "epic." And yet, as epic-like as Gertie and her story are, Arnow does not make her larger than her Earth-home.

Gertie cooks, plants, harvests, preserves, stores, soothes, heals, bears, nurtures, and at one point even performs a successful emergency tracheotomy on her son Amos. She does these things quietly and in the rhythms of the universe. She is truly indigenous to her environment because she sees the Earth as a living being and she a part of that Earth: She threw in some fallen dead apple limbs and a few sand rocks, whispering as she walked away, "That'll hold back a little dirt, an keep this hillside from bleeden [sic] to death" (52–3). Her particular fondness for trees comes out when she smiles at an old hickory: "You'd be good an [sic] tough . . . an yer heart wood's dead, but I'll leave you for seed an hicker nuts fer th squirrels an my youngens." (137)

Water for Gertie comes from streams, not faucets: "The water, cold with faint tastes of earth and iron and moss and the roots of trees, was like other drinks from other springs, the first step upward in the long stairs of the day; everything before it, was night; everything after, day." (81) When she goes to check on her father's farm, "the ragged, uncut hay fields, the pasture, empty of cattle . . . all cried out to her that her father was old, with a crippled leg, and that Henley was dead." (60) Earth speaks to Gertie as clearly as Clovis, the children, and her mother speak to her. The language is different, but Earth speaks to her nonetheless. Earth is living; Earth gives to Gertie her reason for being, and Gertie in her epic-like proportions, gives fully back to Earth.

Just outside these sacred places of farm and woods where Gertie feels a rootedness lies a space profane, and in that space is where Gertie loses her connection to Earth. It is not physical space; it is more like a way of life, and it involves Gertie's relationship to her mother. Her mother is her authority figure; when Gertie's mother gives her orders, Gertie listens and follows them, even though she knows, consciously, that to do so weakens her connection to her Self and Earth. Her mother has her convinced that she speaks for God. The God of Gertie's and her mother's upbringing is punitive, unpredictable, usually angry, and violent. (62) These adjectives can also be applied to Gertie's mother. This mother/daughter relationship turns out to be the catalyst for Gertie's future decisions, and the outcome will permanently uproot Gertie.

With the strong ties to nature that Gertie feels, it can be difficult to understand how Gertie's mother holds a stronger influence over Gertie than her beloved Earth. However, I see Gertie's mother as more than her mother; she is her upbringing. As much as Gertie loves nature and all that it gives to her, including her life, the fundamental Christian patriarchal approach to life that every one of her family and neighbors have been infused with for generations can not overcome what Gertie knows in her heart is the truth about the universe. In her conversations with her mother, Gertie is the child again. The child that Gertie was, was a child raised as a sinner in the hands of an angry God: "Th [sic] Lord thy God am a terrible God" [said her mother to Gertie]. (62) When a child is raised like that by family, church, and neighborhood, it is difficult to break that mold of living; in Gertie's childhood—pre-war, and place—the hills of Kentucky, where families were easily isolated due to lack of communicative devices like telephones, newspapers, and schools, it was next to impossible for Gertie to break the mold. If she could have gone away to college . . . but Gertie did not even have an elementary school to go to. Neither do her children. She teaches them to read from the Bible, the Constitution, and books of poetry, as her father taught her.

Gertie does have her own ideas and beliefs; that we know by her response to anything from the Earth—from carving a doll for Cassie Marie out of a piece of hickory wood to the drink from the spring that tasted of moss and roots. But going against the way everyone else lives in an area that would keep track of everything she—and everyone else—did would be very difficult.

Her mother tells her that she is "mighty close to bein' a infedel." (65) Mrs. Kendrick does not realize how close to the truth she comes. For Gertie, "Her foundation was not on God but what God had promised Moses—land." (128) Land. Gertie is saving for the fifteen years since she and Clovis were married to buy her own piece of land. She has been saving egg money, selling walnuts and firewood, keeping out pennies and nickels from the money Clovis gives her for supplies, and then from her brother's inheritance received after he was killed in the war. She cannot inherit her father's land because she was born female. Being the surviving older daughter is not enough. For Gertie's mother, when Henley dies in the war, "he had taken with him the Kendrick name, the Kendrick land." (71) Gertie's mother is going to sell the land because her husband has an injured leg. She could have deeded the farm to Gertie, but she will not because, according to Mrs. Kendrick, females do not own land.

Why does Gertie's mother wield so much power? The root of *power* is from the Medieval English *pouer* and the Latin *potere*, meaning "to be able." If power is taken and used as control over another, that is really domination, not power used in its root sense. The "power" of Mrs. Kendrick, then, is domination.

A balanced meaning of power is to see it as a force that comes from within, a life-giving and life-sustaining energy that allows a person "to be able." In its best sense, power comes from within; it neither diminishes another person, nor is it diminished by the power/energy of another. This latter definition does not fit Gertie's mother. It does fit Gertie.

We will never unearth the root cause of why Mrs. Kendrick is so dominating; Harriette Arnow does not provide that information. We do know that, according to Mrs. Kendrick, she married "a weak and pitiful man." (71) Mr. Kendrick, the parent to whom Gertie confided, was too cowed by his wife to speak out for what he

thought right, especially if it went against how his wife had inter-
preted a situation. Mrs. Kendrick is weaker in physical health in
her early and mid-married years than Gertie. That physical weakness, combined with her marriage to a "pitiful man" who could not
make much of a living from their farm for them, perhaps turns
Gertie's mother to controlling the only thing left in her life to control: Gertie. Gertie would have been born about 1912 or so, in the
hills of Kentucky, to a poor but intelligent farm wife—maybe even
artistic—her husband, "pitiful"; the wife gave birth to a female,
Gertie, that almost killed her in childbirth. This scenario has created more than one dominating mother in the mother/ daughter
relationship. (Remember Sally Carrighar's birth.) A son could leave
and make a life on his own. So could a younger sister, especially
since the older sister was settled in near the parents. Gertie, as
elder daughter/older sister could not.

Gertie, in turn, accommodates her mother because of the
time and place and circumstances into which she, Gertie, was
born. Added to that is the constant reminder of the childbirth experience; constantly reminding a child that she nearly killed her
mother in the process of being born is a harsh burden to carry.
Combining that knowledge with the word of God, as taught by the
minister and Mrs. Kendrick, does not allow Gertie to form her own
identity that represents her Self. As long as Gertie is not near her
mother, she is all right. Physical presence throws Gertie into the
dependent role of the child, the good child, disciplined to obey an
authority figure for fear of eternal damnation. (60-75)

Although born near where Gertie was born, and raised near
where Gertie was raised, Clovis has always hated farming and anything to do with earth and land. His love is for anything mechanical; he tinkers with car motors, sometimes even taking one apart
only to reassemble it later. He is called up for his Army exam (the
story begins in 1944), but he is rejected. (He is too old, being past
thirty.) He sees the rejection as a chance to do what he has always
wanted to do: work with things mechanical. So instead of return-

ing home after the rejection, he journeys to Detroit and immediately finds a job in one of the factories that makes parts for the war effort. His first letter to Gertie after the move is to tell her to bring the family to Detroit. Of course Gertie wants to stay in Kentucky and keep saving for her piece of land.

When Clovis writes and asks her to join him in Detroit, she does not go. When Mrs. Kendrick hears that Gertie bought some land and is not planning to take the family to Detroit to live with Clovis, no matter that the conditions are more wretched there than in Kentucky, she berates her daughter in front of her grandchildren: "Oh, Lord, . . . sh's [sic] turned her own children against their father. She's never taught them th [sic] Bible where it says, 'Leave all else an [sic] cleave to thy husband.' She's never read to them th words write by Paul, 'Wives, be in subjection unto your husband, as unto th Lord.'" (141)

This passage creates a major turning point for Gertie; it appears that Gertie has the same weakness her father has. Instead of speaking up for their farm and her family, she gives in to her mother with silence, the silence of the good girl: "Gertie opened her mouth, closed it." (143) Reuben, the eldest at twelve years watches, and "his glance fixed on his mother's face was filled with the contempt of the strong for the weak." (143)

Never again in the story will Gertie see the hills of Kentucky, smell the pine, the cedar, "the good clean air," see the Little Dipper and tell Cassie Marie that the Little Dipper is speaking to her, saying: "if'n you lost all yer friends an kin, you'd still have us [the stars] an th sun an th moon." (124) In Detroit, the sky is so full of smog that Gertie and Cassie Marie never see the stars. Never again will she make lard out of a pig she raised and slaughtered, make bread from meal she grew, and serve butter she churned from the milk of her cow.

Old John tells Gertie: "I cain't let a piece a land come atween a woman an her man an *her people*" [emphasis mine]. (145) "Her people" is metonymy for the mother, her history, her heritage.

Gertie's father is in favor of Gertie buying the land. Old John is in favor of Gertie buying his land until Gertie's mother reminds him with the Biblical quote, "Wives, be in subjection to your husbands" that he will be in sinful compliance if he sells his land to Gertie.

Old John quickly interprets "her people" to be Gertie's mother, to the exclusion of her father. Otherwise, he would not have given the money back to Gertie since her father was in favor of the transaction. Thus Mrs. Kendrick uses the accepted interpretation of particular Christian beliefs to distort the power structure of her extended family.

Clovis would be all right only if he can stay in Detroit and work in a factory. He exists in the world of industry, of mechanical things. That is his real love—not farming, not clear air, not water that tastes of moss and roots. His world is found under the hood of a car. When he finally writes to Gertie, it is to tell her to come to Detroit because he has a place for her and the kids.

The area in Detroit where he has found them a place is described as follows: "The redness trembled like light from a flame, as if somewhere far away, a piece of hell had come up from underground." (168) This is the world/ kingdom of Clovis. He is happy.

The web of life is only as strong as the strands the form it. If any of the strands break, that weakens the web. In this story, several strands from the web break from its center, entangle around other strands, while others hang limply in space. Clovis's strand breaks and hangs on limply. He does not overtly harm others, and he is not aware of the damage his decision carries to want Gertie and the children to come to Detroit. Life in Kentucky for Gertie becomes decentered and unbalanced because the strands representing her mother and Old John break and entangle with Gertie's; the force is too strong for hers to hold to the center.

Obviously, Gertie's mother is not a woman who loves the Earth as does Gertie or she would be more tuned to earth and its cycles. Her strand in the web of life would be rooted in the seasons. She is the negative side of motherhood, the side that, if it not acknowledged and dealt with, becomes devouring. Mrs. Kendrick pretends to be the good wife/mother who does Clovis's bidding in his absence, only because it suits her ends. She goes to Old John to have him recant the land deal with Gertie so that Clovis's and her wish could be granted. These actions against Gertie entangle and eventually uproot the web of life in Kentucky from its moorings. Gertie is caught in the uprootedness.

Lest this seem too harsh a picture of Gertie's mother, remember the times and the circumstances into which Mrs. Kendrick was born. Like many poor white women born when Mrs. Kendrick was born—late 1800s—reared as she was, one of the few tactics she could use to control her circumstances was to quote passages from the Bible about authority and domination. I do not explore her character to be harsh or judgmental; I explore her character because she could step out of the pages of this story and exist on our level of reality, as could her daughter. Like her daughter, she speaks to truths about certain kinds of Indo-European women existing, certainly, in the context of the history of the United States during the war and post-war period. There were many women, at least in the small communities like Gertie's who had no other way to find their identity than to try to dominate the helpless in the name of the Lord. Harriette Arnow did not create these characters from nothing.

While Gertie and her five children are riding the smoke-filled, body-crammed train to Detroit, she has lots of time to think. One of those passages expressing her thoughts is particularly intriguing, especially in the light of feminist theory. In this passage, she positions herself against four dominant authority figures during a time in our history when (most) women were treated as invisible in society: her mother, though female, carries authority because/when she speaks for God; God Himself as a male image and thus an ongoing authority figure; Clovis, her husband to whom she was to subject herself at all times; and Old John, owner of a great deal of land and thus naturally a male:

She was a coward, worse than any of the others. If she could have stood up to her mother and God and Clovis and Old John, she'd have been in her own house this night. Oh, if she were back with the money in her pocket, she'd say No to them all and move to her farm, sin or no. (148–49)

But she will not speak out; she has been trained too well to be the good girl. To the last word of the story, she will not say "No." She will remain silent, and she will do what she is told.

The train ride to Detroit physically severs Gertie from her roots in Kentucky and throws her into a fragmented, alienating, and thus physically profane space, because it is devoid of all sense of her ties to the universe. Detroit is another reality to her; indeed, it is "as if somewhere far away a piece of hell had come up from underground." (168) She moves from heaven ("Jesus walks th earth, an we're goen to have us a little piece a heaven right here on earth") (77), to hell. How she copes with this new layer of reality will decide whether she can root herself again. She will not be able to root herself in land; there is none. But if she can root herself in her Self, then she can begin the healing process to wholeness.

Gertie in Detroit

Once Gertie reaches Detroit, she assumes the role that Tillie Olsen calls "the essential angel." Olsen defines women in this role as those who "contend . . . [with] the physical responsibilities for daily living, for the maintenance of life."[12] To Olsen this angel is so lowly that she is all but absent from the actual content of most men's books, "except perhaps on the dedication page: *To my wife, without whom . . .* [sic]"[13]

Olsen had another name for essential angels; she called them "honey drudgers: the winged unmiraculous [. . .] [living the] whirled mother-maintenance life, that most women, not privileged, know."[14] Harriette Arnow was one, notes Olsen. So, she writes, were Mary Austin, Susan Glaspell, Agnes Smedley and Sylvia Plath. As wives they were essential angels; as writers they wrote of them, when they could find some uninterrupted moments to do so.

Arnow's "angel," Gertie, is a woman of enormous talent. Had she been a woman of the '90s, instead of the '40s, a woman with access to a phone and a newspaper, she would have, at least, recognized that what she whittled was art. She could still be an essential angel in the '90s, but she would at least have insight as to why she is the one interrupted when she is whittling and Clovis is not when he is dismantling a car engine. But she is a woman of the '40s, with no access to communications, and she lives in a culture where disobeying her mother's values, that are really God's values, is unthinkable. So she goes to Detroit as an essential angel.

The change of place does not erase Gertie's innate human drive to create and love beauty. Although Gertie possesses the other innate human drives that Olsen lists: "intellect, organization, invention, sense of justice . . . courage . . . resilience, resistance, need for community,"[15] she will be denied the opportunity to bring those drives to fullness. Some, like resilience and courage, will keep her from despair when she realizes that her family will not return to Kentucky when the war is over; Clovis loves the factories in Detroit and the motorized gadgets to such an extent that he would buy them even though the family might go without decent food for some days, *and* that that act would be acceptable to the community. Others, like the need to create beauty, will die when she splits her beloved piece of cherry wood into pieces large enough to mass-produce jigsawed dolls; her sense of justice smothered when Clovis is involved in killing a man, killing him with her whittling knife. And Gertie continues to cook and wash and baby-sit neighbor children . . . and live in fear that her children will come to harm in Detroit.

Her fear is well-founded, of course. Amos, Enoch and Clytie adjust all too easily to the area, though Gertie does not want them to adjust to a place where there is not even one tree "for the children to see come spring," thus losing their connection with the Kentucky hills. In contrast, her oldest, Reuben, does not adjust; to escape adjustment he runs away back to their beloved hill country in Kentucky to live with her mother. Cassie Marie, her youngest daughter, dies a slow, painful death after being run over by a train.

It is Cassie Marie's death that brings Gertie to the understanding that it will be years before she will see Kentucky again, if ever. She has done her best to transplant herself from Kentucky to the Detroit projects; she does more than her best to hold her family together when there is, literally, no earth on which to send down roots and hold them firmly. The day Cassie dies, Gertie, still covered in Cassie's blood, "sniffed the blood-crusted sleeve so close to her face. She sprang up, looking wildly about her as she lived again the losing battles—all the battles: to have the land, to make Reuben happy, to reach Cassie—and the last big battle—to hold the blood—nothing left to lose." (417) Nowhere in the first quarter of the book—the Kentucky setting—is life a battle for Gertie, losing or otherwise. She does not think in war words. Gertie does not see life as a battle until Detroit; she sees life as a dance with the earth, the song played out to the rhythms of the universe, "shaped by the needs of the land and the animals swinging through the seasons." (210)

The best that Gertie can do to maintain her sanity and keep the family functioning in the place she sees as hell is to daydream, to remember and recall. As she makes sandwiches at 6 a.m., she remembers milking time, "or the early morning trip to the spring." (209) As she walks the children to school, snow under their boots, "her corn and fodder were in the barn . . . her red cedar churn filled with clabbered cream." (221) These memories, held to tenaciously, keep her going on, though in Detroit, she is ruled and dominated by clock time: the "ticking voice boss[ing] her that pushed her through . . . all her work, her meals and her sleep." (210) It is "the voice of the thing that had jerked Henley from the land [and] put

Clovis in Detroit." (210) For Gertie, clock time is in total contradiction to the earth's seasons and to the farm's cycles she lovingly gave herself over to in Kentucky. Yet she obeys the voice of the clock. Why? Does the clock replace her mother as God? Is the clock the God of the industrialized world? The clock was invented by men, and yet the very men who invented it became its slaves. And the women, too. How could that happen to someone like Gertie, who, for over thirty years had danced with the rhythms of the universe?

The day that Cassie dies, Gertie approaches Clovis about taking Cassie's body home to Kentucky; Clovis says no, he would not take Cassie's body home to be buried in the family graveyard: "—they'd be th train ride there—an back an—." (417) Clovis will never live in Kentucky again; he adjusted to Detroit. Gertie's plea to "—take her back amongst her kin" (417) falls on deaf ears. Even though to be buried in the family graveyard is more than a physical act to Gertie, she obeys the voice of Clovis, because the voice of Clovis is the voice of God. And yet, being with kin in death is as vital as being with kin in life. Gertie is caught in a conflict of choosing between profane space—the Detroit graveyard—and sacred space—the family cemetery back in Kentucky. She knows which choice she should make, which choice is natural for her, but it is not the choice that she will make. In Detroit, Gertie is not centered in her Self. She is "governed and driven by the obligations of an existence incorporated into an industrial society."[16]

Gertie both understands and lives "kinship." Clovis does not. "Kin" to Gertie, is the same term as the one Old John uses ("people") when he returns Gertie her money for the land. She should be with her people he says. To Gertie, her people are her kin, and her kin are in Kentucky. To Gertie, Clovis was never "her people"; Clovis is the man she marries and the man who fathers her children. Her ties to the earth are more important to her than her ties to Clovis. The earth is kin; Clovis is not. Kin is what is sacred to Gertie. But Clovis speaks for God, and God has the power to condemn her to Hell for all eternity, for heaven-knows-what. Gertie certainly does not know. If she did, she would be able to say "No" to her mother and to Clovis because she would know that their interpretation of God's word through the Bible is not necessarily the appropriate interpretation for her.

Seated near Cassie's coffin at the funeral parlor, Gertie "sat still and straight . . . eyes . . . bewildered as a lost child's eyes . . . who even as it begs to find the way home, knows there is no finding the way, for home, and all other things at the end of the way were also lost." (418) The spiritual harmony, relationship, balance and dignity that had once informed her life are shattered, fragmented.

It seems that Gertie can sink no further. Her days are "like a long grey thing sliding past, tight like a tunnel, but she must somehow squeeze through." (421) After Cassie's death, Hell changes from belching smoke-stacks and flames of fire reaching the stars when the steel workers pour the molds, to a long grey thing sliding past.

Why is Gertie in Hell, anyway? According to the Christian doctrine she was taught, Hell is for sinners, grave sinners who commit grave sins. What grave sin has Gertie committed? That she loves the universe more than her husband? That her mother almost dies when she is born? That she is born female? Or, like Lot's wife, that she looked back not when she boarded the train to Detroit, but in her dreaming and remembering, always dreaming of the day they would return to heaven on earth. Then is that her sin? That she did look back?

If, indeed, Gertie's sin is that she looks back, she learns her lesson. Her last dream to return to Kentucky comes as Cassie is buried in a cemetery about six blocks from the projects. The war is over. Men and women are laid off by the hundreds at the Flint plants, so the remaining employees are going to strike. That means that Clovis will be out of work soon because he will support the strike. Gertie takes refuge in the small area that is a bedroom and remembers: she recalls Dock, her faithful mule; food in the barn for winter; the land she owned for fewer than twenty-four hours where all her children would be safe.

> To live that way, without debts, unions, boys in cars, foremen, traffic; to be free from the fears—forever at her back. . . . She had never cried for Cassie, but now she cried for a mule that wouldn't recollect her, but with him she had been so free, so unafraid. (524)

From that moment on to the story's end, Gertie will neither dream nor recall again.

A thread that runs through the weave of *The Dollmaker* is Gertie's fascination with finding the perfect face to carve into her block of cherry wood—wood from a tree that grew on the land in Kentucky. Even though it is heavy and awkward, she has it shipped up to Detroit.

While in Kentucky Gertie would take odd moments to work on her block of cherry wood. When the Army men ask what she could make from the wood, she tells them: "I thought on Christ—but somehow his face ain't never clear . . . maybe Judas." The officer looks at her suspiciously, and she explains that "it wasn't the 'drooly' Judas, "his hand held out fer the silver, but the Judas who gave the money back. But they's not many like him gives th money away an feels sorry onct they've got it." (23)

The first encounter with money that causes Gertie to think about Judas occurs when a lady on the train to Detroit pays Gertie for a basket that Gertie makes out of a hickory nut. "Pay fer whittlen foolishness!" is Gertie's first response. It is one thing to exchange eggs or firewood for money. That money is means to an end, the end being her own land, so that all of what she raised stayed with the family; half of everything would not go to the landowner. But to be paid for "whittlen foolishness" is a concept totally foreign to Gertie, except when she thought of why Judas took the thirty pieces of silver. The experience of taking a dollar for a doll is a foreshadowing of the role that money will play for her and her children in Detroit. She will ponder Judas more and more when selling her "whittlen foolishness" becomes the only way to gain money to buy groceries to feed her family. Clovis feels no obligation to give her food money on a regular basis.

It is Cassie Marie, Gertie's second youngest, who gives the first clue to the reader that Gertie is looking in the wrong place for the face on the cherry wood. Cassie Marie has been lying on the floor in her home in Kentucky kicking the wood absentmindedly when Gertie tells her to stop before she ruins it: "I fergot she could feel it, Mom." 'Him.' Gertie said. . . . 'Her.' Cassie said." (47) Cassie wants her mother to carve the hair into braids. "Take her out, Mom . . . she wants out. She's been a waiten there so long . . . ever since I was little." Gertie's reply is: "Way before then. . . . He's been a waiten there in the wood you might say since before I was born . . . one of these days . . . we'll find the time an a face fer him an bring him out a that block." (48)

Notice the word "time" in the one statement Gertie makes. She will find time and a face. In Kentucky, though she was happy when she was outside working in the dirt, the earth, Gertie did not have much time to do things for herself, such as carving on the piece of cherry wood. She would carve for others—the handles and dolls—but not take time to do what nourished *her* Self. She was the essential angel sometimes even in Kentucky—doing for others because someone has to maintain life, particularly if that someone is born into poverty and not privilege. In a passage where Gertie is visiting her mother, she ponders her life as a Kendrick: that in the little spare time Gertie had had from the farm work, she used the time to whittle.

But she whittles with guilt. "Once during the middle of the afternoon, she found herself kneeling by it, knife open in her hand. She sprang up, ashamed of her time-wasting ways." (88)

Gertie has two dreams while in Kentucky, two desires: one is to carve the face on the wood and the second one is to own her own land, for "with her own land she'd never have to feel guilty about wasting time." Owning something that belongs to her, that she has worked hard and long to buy, is as important as carving the face. It appears that Gertie equates ownership with freedom from guilt, perhaps even free from her mother's hold on her in terms of religious values.

Even in Detroit, Gertie holds onto her dream of owning land; she tells Clovis: "But a body's got a right to be free. They oughtn't to have to belong to nothen, not even a union." (530) To Gertie, the union is like a landlord—owner of another's soul. Gertie does not want to own land for profit and gain; land is not one of the spoils of war to her. Gertie is not a soldier out to conquer. Owning land means freedom, freedom to work with the land, to have it yield its potential, not to have it yield more than it can bear to feed her family and the landlord's as well. Owning the land will help her "be beholden to no man, not even to Clovis." (139)

Gertie cannot fulfill her desire to own land in Detroit, but she can carve the face on the cherry wood. The wood does not arrive for a while, so she busies herself carving dolls and animals. They come easily to her, even though she treats the smaller pieces of wood the same way she treats her larger piece: with tenderness and care, acknowledging that these small pieces have spirits in them, too. In one instance, with a piece of maple, harder and finer grained than any she had known, Gertie begins to whittle in the time before the children were to be called for school. "Little by little, by Friday morning [the hen] was there waiting in the wood for the knife to free her, a good hen, ready to lay many eggs." (210)

When the wood arrives, Gertie begins again to hunt for the face in her lean moments of spare time. However, after Cassie dies, Gertie quits working on the face—the face that haunts her by not appearing. She works on the hands. As the days pass, as the war comes to an end, as her children adjust, as the unions go on strike, she works on the hands. Once in a while she works on the mantle that lies on the shoulders, maybe a bit on the hair. Then back to the hands. The hands that show themselves through the wood are cupped, one above the other as if the lower hand holds something. Would that hand give back what was in it, or would the upper hand come down over the lower hand to keep what was there? "Was he just getting or just giving away?" What is in the lower hand? These are the questions that bother Gertie; "the answer[s] were not in her head, but something for the knife to find, like the face buried in the wood." (477) Until she sees the face she can not get the hands right. Still, she works on the hands.

Another question that emerges: does art shape reality or does reality shape art? Gertie does not begin to work on the hands until she moves to Detroit, and after she has the experience of taking money for whittling. There is a moment when she decides that the hands are exchanging money and the figure is Judas: "for days she's been wanting to finish the lifted hand that lingered longingly above the money in the other hand; for it was money—taken—but soon to be given away. The man, then was Judas. . . . Christ had no money, just his life." (564)

Gertie's hands begin to form the same pattern as the hands in the wood as her lower hand "opening now into a cupped palm, thumb and finger pinched together over two one-dollar bills and a fifty cent piece." (573) She sells one of the jigsaw dolls Clovis mass-produces in their Detroit home to a policeman, and he pays her. She sells another doll to a grocer.

When her neighbor Mrs. Anderson comes to visit her, Mrs. Anderson's point of view on the hands is, "he won't keep still and hold it. He'll give it back." "'A body cain't allers give back—things,' Gertie said, filled suddenly with a tired despair; the wood was Judas after all." (585) However, this Judas is not the same Judas that Gertie described to the Army officer: the Judas that *would* give back because he was sorry to have gotten it. Gertie is very hard on herself; her scrupulosity over taking responsibility for everything that seems tainted is hard for me, as a reader, to bear. And yet, I do bear it, because it was a scrupulosity with which I and the other females who were reared in my church were taught. Thus the sadness that comes over me when I read of Gertie's struggles in Detroit is one borne of affiliation with her inability to know that she has a sacred Self that is valuable. She is more than the sum of her parts: essential angel, honey drudger, Biblical wife, renter, blameful daughter, clock keeper. Her strand in the web of life is as integral to the health of that web as is the tree that produced her piece of cherry wood or the parents that produced Clovis.

The evening before she takes her piece of cherry wood to the scrap-wood lot to have it cut into boards for jigsaw dolls, she works feverishly on the unfinished palm of the uplifted hand, then on a line in the down-turning palm. Arnow places Gertie's feverish carving against a less cyclical and seasonal but nonetheless real background. It is not the background of molasses-making and dogwood blossoms, the background of milking and churning, the background of hay in the barn and food in the cellar for winter. It is a city background, with its own cycles and seasons:

> The children went to bed and Clovis went to bed, but she worked on. Victor went to the steel mill, Whit came home from the bowling alley, the fast passenger train that had always used to waken the children with its long screech for the crossing, passed, and still she worked. . . . The late autumn dawn was still far away, but the dead time of night had come, when the traffic on the through street was thinned to single cars passing . . . before she . . . dropped the knife into her pocket and went to bed. (595–96)

In the morning Gertie and Amos, not yet in school all day, go to the scrap-wood lot where her beloved piece of cherry wood is chopped into pieces.

Why Gertie sacrifices the one thing that in Detroit gives her any sense of her connection to the land, her history, her self is not clear. I think it is because Gertie cannot admit to herself that the face in the block of wood is not Christ; it is not Judas; it is not even any of the neighbors in the alley, any one of whom "would ha done." (599) The face in the block of wood is her face.

Gertie cannot find her face in the wood because she cannot find her own face. A face gives a person an identity. Gertie does not yet have an identity. For all her wisdom as an Earth Woman, for all her patience as a mother, for all her intelligence about the Bible and the Constitution, for all her understanding about the seasons and their cycles, for all her need for ownership of land to not be "beholden," Gertie has not found her own identity, her own power, her own Self. Her mother "owned" a large part of Gertie's Self, her children—particularly her dead Cassie and her runaway Reuben—another part, clock time another part. Who is Gertie? Gertie does not know because she is a woman "governed and driven." She has an inclusive and connective spirituality to all that is living; however, in that inclusion, her identity is not discrete.

She has insight, however. After Cassie dies and Gertie is near madness, she lashes out at little Amos, screaming, "'I didn't send her off to be killed. I didn't aim to kill her when Mom made me come. It was Mom an—' . . . No, not her mother, herself, herself,—only, she couldn't say it. She ought to have stood up to them all—." (421–22)

The insight, however, is not enough to enable her to find her face in the wood. As Gertie's story unfolds, it is her "tonguelessness" at critical moments in her life that does not allow her to act on what she wants for herself. That inability to act for the good of herself, and her children, is not something she can control. The times into which she was born and her economic circumstances were against her using the voice that would speak for her Self. In those times, Gertie was not a strand in the web of life; she was a fly, caught, wrapped up, and in time psychologically devoured.

Thus, she would have her piece of cherry wood split into pieces to make dolls. Why? Mrs. Anderson gave her fifty dollars to make dolls for the women in Grosse Pointe, a wealthy suburb of Detroit. Why? Clovis needs the money for a truck payment. Why?

The family needs more food and Clovis is on strike. Why? She no longer dreams and she no longer recalls. So like the essential angel, she does what she has to do to maintain the life for herself and her children—and husband—even if it means denying an innate human drive to create beauty, to transform a piece of wood, grown as a tree on her father's land before she was born, into a face that contains force and energy and life-giving power: the face that would be her Self.

When Gertie splits the wood at the scrap-wood lot, she splits herself. As she splits the wood-that-is-herself, "the wood cried out. . . . The wood, straight-grained and true, came apart with a crying rendering sound." (599)

At the very end of the story, she tells the wood lot man that "they's millions an millions a faces plenty fine enough—fer him." (599) Yes, "fer him," if the face in the wood had been a "him," It was not; it was a "her." Until Gertie realizes that Cassie was right, until she discovers that she was creating her own face, in whatever form that takes, she will remain split like her piece of wood, and she will not heal.

Mrs. Anderson: portrait of an angel

As Harriette Arnow did not create characters like Gertie's mother from nothing, neither did Mrs. Anderson and her family, one set of Gertie's neighbors in the Detroit projects, come from nothing. Born and reared in the hills of Kentucky, Arnow also had first-hand experience with the projects in Detroit: she lived there with her husband and children during and after World War II. The projects living taught her much:

"Here . . . regardless of our background, [we] have a common bond. We are human beings. . . . All of us . . . wives with children . . . uprooted to follow our husbands to Detroit. . . . We [talked] . . . of the war, our children . . . , our babies, and often of flowers. . . .

We grew to know each other better than those who study 'the
migrant' by statistics built in direct questioning can ever
know."[17]

Gertie is in the projects about a month before she learns that
her neighbor Mrs. Anderson paints; one of the other neighbors
tells Gertie, "'You two outghta git together. Mrs. Anderson paints
pitchers.' [sic] Mrs. Anderson . . . shifted the baby to her other arm.
'Not any more. There just isn't time or space—here.'"

Time and space. Both disappear for Mrs. Anderson when she
and her family move to the projects from Muncie, Indiana, and she,
too, falls into the role of Olsen's essential angel. She, too, desires to
return to the farm they left behind—that they own—the way
Gertie desires to return to Kentucky. She, like Gertie, thinks that
she will be going back when the war is over. Going back home is the
dream she holds on to when she is unable to paint in the projects.
(283)

Like Gertie, she does not feel that she belongs in the projects,
but for a different reason. Mrs. Anderson (and she is called "Mrs.
Anderson") believes that she and her family are better than the
other families because her husband Homer (and he is called
"Homer") is a college graduate. Though they live in the projects
only to allow her husband to make his observations and collect his
data for his dissertation on the "migrants" who live there, Mrs.
Anderson is also part of her husband's experiment, as are their two
children. Thus the despair in her voice comes from more than not
having enough time and space to paint. It comes from being cast
into the same role as the other women who live near them; Mrs.
Anderson knows that she is a statistic, like the other women—a
part of the collected data—no better than the others; her children,
too, are statistics and thus seen by their father in the same way he
views the other children: no better than. Added to the insult of
being considered "the same as," Homer Anderson is having Mrs.
Anderson rear the children according to theories he collects from

other experiments. Though their economic and educational circumstances are better than Gertie's, there is no way that this husband and wife have an equal relationship. Because she is female, she is not allowed a voice either.

To soften the blow of losing her identity as a person to the projects, to industrial Detroit, and to her husband, like many of her neighbors in the alley, she begins to drink. Later she will turn to prescription drugs when the drinking does not dull the pain of loneliness and loss.

Gertie comes to understand her enigmatic neighbor as she, Gertie, has less time and almost no space to carve the piece of cherry wood. Gertie's time with her block of wood erodes when she takes a new job: whittling dolls and hens and boats and crucifixes for the wealthy of Grosse Point. Homer brings her the orders from his bosses in the office where he works.

The incident that gave Gertie the feeling of sisterhood with Mrs. Anderson is the night that Clovis, for the first time since they were married, tries to order Gertie around, "as if she were a mule" for having made a fuss with Reuben's teacher over Reuben's inability to adjust to his classroom, the school, Detroit. Back home in Kentucky Gertie did her share, "maybe more than her share of feeding and fending for the family. . . . Here everything, even to the kindling wood, came from Clovis. She understood in one second of time so many things—the trapped look in Mrs. Anderson's eyes." (338) Mrs. Anderson is stuck, and she hungers to feed that part of her being—the Self—that calls for beauty, art, justice, resistance. Her paints and her canvases once fed that Self, but she has not even picked up a brush since the move to Detroit. Olsen quotes Jane Bowles: "In the 20 years that we've lived here (Morocco), I have written only two short stories and nothing else. It's good for Paul, but not for me."[18] This is also the fate of both Mrs. Anderson and Gertie. Their husbands are happy; they are not.

A year passes before Mrs. Anderson brings up painting again in conversation with Gertie; they are discussing baby food. She says to Gertie that, "if I could paint with strained baby foods I might get famous. The tints would be something unknown in nature and as yet unconceived by man." Mrs. Anderson is blocking from her mind the desire, the dream to paint because her husband is climbing the corporate ladder, and she is cast in the role of enabler to assist his climbing. There is no time to paint, let alone space where her materials can be stored safely.

After Cassie dies and Gertie is unable to make her pieces of reality fit together, Mrs. Anderson takes upon herself the task of filling Gertie's emptiness with the phenobarbitol that fills *her* emptiness. Gertie takes the pink medicine for a while, then she refuses it and instead turns to her block of wood for solace. Gertie's refusal is a turning point for Mrs. Anderson in that she finally begins to unfold to Gertie her love for painting and her admiration for Gertie's ability to carve. "'You must finish it—finish it,'" said Mrs. Anderson to Gertie, "as if the finishing of it were a job that could be done only with great sacrifice and determination. 'I aim to—allus I aimed to finish him, but never had the time. But now, seems like, they's nothen left tu me—but—time—an she allus begged me. I wish I'd tuck th time.'" Mrs. Anderson replies, "'But how does one take the time when—' Mrs. Anderson . . . [then] dropped all in a heap on the floor, bent her forehead against a wooden shoulder, and wept fully and completely." The moment brings Mrs. Anderson to a low point of despair as she continues: "'—why raise children? Why give your life up to them—everything— if—if their lives will be as miserable as your own? Why?'" (438–39)

Interestingly, Gertie will make a similar cry before story's end when she asks herself, "What was the good of trying to keep your own if when they grew up their days were like your own— changeovers and ugly painted dolls?" (503–04) Thus, it is through her friendship with Mrs. Anderson that Gertie attains insights into the human condition that she never would have attained had she remained in Kentucky. However, had she stayed in Kentucky, her creative spirit would not have been crushed. The polarity in the opposing forces of Kentucky/Detroit, creator/essential angel bring the conflict of Gertie's life as well as her growth as a human being to the cutting edge of paradox.

Gertie's emphasis, however, is slightly different from Mrs. Anderson's; Mrs. Anderson's emphasis is on the sacrifices by the mother that go into rearing children while the husband/father is making his way in the world: the loss of the wife's/mother's talents, drives, and dreams. Gertie's words question keeping her children near her and with her until adulthood and beyond if, in the rearing, she has no influence. But never once does Gertie wish she never had children; her children are her life. Seeing Amos, Clytie, and Enoch adjust to the alleys of the projects and the values of industrial Detroit, losing Cassie to the trainyards and Reuben to Kentucky—those are the matters of Gertie's despair, not having given birth to them.

Mrs. Anderson finally confesses to Gertie that she wishes she had painted some of the neighbors in the alley: "Do you know that all these months I've lived here . . . and collected statistics for Homer I've ached inside to go on with my painting . . . the grey houses and the dirty trash cans, always spilling, and the black steelmill smoke . . . and the clean silvery airplanes." Even the child Wheateye, "dirty with popsicle juice dribbling down her chin . . . stand[ing] on the coalhouse" (440–41) to help Mrs. Anderson count airplanes for Homer's thesis is food for the artist in her. "This alley could keep a thousand artists busy a thousand years— and now there'll never be any time—it takes time to be a pillar of society." (472)

In her collection of essays, Alice Walker discovers just what Mrs. Anderson discovers: "while thinking about the far-reaching world . . . , often the truest answer to a question that really matters can be found very close."[19] It wasn't for her to paint angels and mountains; it was for her to paint Wheateye and the alleys and the Detroit night sky during a "pour."

Harriette Arnow paints us a picture with words of a woman who learns too late where to find some of those answers: close. The Anderson family moves to the wealthy Detroit suburb of Grosse Point, and Mrs. Anderson knows that she will never paint at all once they move to their new house and become "pillars of society." The tragedy of Mrs. Anderson's life—and it is a tragedy because she has gained some understanding and thus has the opportunity to heed the call to healing—is that not only does she know that she will not paint again, "I must quit *wanting* [emphasis mine] to paint." She lets go of the dream, the remembering. Her husband has been bought by the Detroit factory executives and so has she, to be the "perfect courtier's wife." (473)

Mrs. Anderson has drifted further into a despair that now is covered over with enough money to make everything look "smooth . . . no rough stuff, at least nothing the public can see. . . . Everything is like that . . . the skinned-onion look . . . smooth, no smell." (586) She lives a lie and, unlike the women Linda Hogan writes about, does not know how to begin to betray that lie. Unlike Gertie, she lacks, now, the *wanting* to paint. The children are "adjusting," the neighbors are "nice"; they "do not let their houses get mussed or [their] children go—well, a shade too grimy—and paint—You don't by any chance have any pink medicine left." (588)

Mrs. Anderson's last encounter with Gertie comes at the end of the story when she returns to the projects to ask Gertie if she would make some dolls and crucifixes for a church bazaar the women of Grosse Point are putting on at Christmastime. (It is now autumn.) In return Mrs. Anderson will give fifty dollars to Gertie in advance, and Gertie would make a commission on each sale. But the ladies of the church want "good wood . . . walnut or cherry or dogwood or holly." (590) Gertie hesitates because she does not know where she can get good wood so late in the year. When she mentions this to Mrs. Anderson, Mrs. Anderson tells Gertie that the woman from Grosse Pointe for whom she is the money bearer realizes this; that is why the advance is so high. As the two woman speak in Gertie's cramped living room, sitting next to them is the piece of half-carved cherry wood.

Fifty dollars or thirty pieces of silver. Both prices buy a living being that was not meant to be turned into a commodity: Judas takes the money and makes Jesus an object for market; Gertie takes the money and commodifies the piece of wood that was her Self.

After Mrs. Anderson puts the fifty dollars into Gertie's hands, she leaves in body, but her spirit in Gertie's life remains; that night is the night that Gertie stays up till almost dawn carving the hands of the figure, the hands that held money. And it is the money from Mrs. Anderson, the money that Clovis saw exchange hands and then took from Gertie to make back payments on his truck, that becomes the catalyst that gives Gertie the idea to split her cherry wood to make the dolls and crucifixes. Though Mrs. Anderson has left the projects, she has not left the context of Gertie's story.

Mrs. Anderson reminds me of Virginia Woolf's angel in the house. Woolf named this construct after a Victorian poem called "The Angel in the House." She is the one who "must charm . . . sympathize . . . flatter . . . conciliate . . . be extremely sensitive to the needs and moods and wishes of others before her own . . . excel in the difficult arts of family life."[20] Like Gertie, she is also a portrait of Tillie Olsen's essential angel, "the angel who must assume the physical responsibilities for daily living, for the maintenance of life," the "instantly interruptable."[21] I do not see Mrs. Anderson surviving her circumstances even in Olsen's sense of the word: as "one who must bear witness to those who foundered; [who tries] to tell how and why it was that they, also worthy of life, did *not* survive."[22] Mrs. Anderson wrestles with Virginia Woolf's angel in the house and Tillie Olsen's essential angel, and the angels win.

Revisioning goddess consciousness in The Fires of Bride
by Ellen Galford

Adrienne Rich sees that the woman writer's journey takes her into the "cratered night of female memory"[23] in order "to retrieve what has been lost, regenerate, reconceive, and give birth."[24] It is in the cratered night that the woman writer finds her mother goddesses and her mother land. Many women artists of all kinds, living or fictive, make this journey. A fictive artist who makes the journey is Maria Milleny, the painter/sculptor in *The Fires of Bride*.[25]

The novel is set in Britain in the 1980s, although the title suggests an older setting. It is a story within a story within a story within a story. The outer story is of a novice television journalist, Lizzie, whose bosses give her the assignment to find material for a documentary on one of the islands in the Outer Hebrides. The station needs a documentary so that its license can be renewed. The men at the station (Lizzie is the only female) suggest "Rediscovering Wimmin's Traditional Culture" as a title so that Lizzie will have to do the story and film; it seems that no one at the station goes to the Outer Hebrides unless forced to do so. The island she is assigned to is called Cailleach, the outermost island of the Outer Hebrides.

In doing research, Lizzie finds that the island's name means "the Crone, the Old Woman. The grey mare, the white sow soaring across the sky."[26] Part of the spiritual history of Cailleach is that the island was created by "the Mother" who "tore off a lump of . . . the earth to form it," scooped up "giant stones in the folds of her apron" and blew them into "sacred circles . . . duns and cairns of the west. Beasts grazing nearby, cows and sheep, always gravitate towards them. But the ungrateful lot who live there light their fires for someone else entirely: Bride, Brigantia, Bridget." (9–10)

Part of Cailleach's sexual history is that the island is so small that "all the women bleed in unison." (10) Part of its political history is that the island really is not Scottish, "a spelling error by a medieval scribe," it is Norwegian.(9)

When Lizzie finally gets to the island, not an easy task, she makes friends with an island innkeeper, Ina Isbister, "a fantastic storyteller" who "tell[s] [the] truth of it, dear." (1) "It" refers to the stone-formed Cailleach Ring, the sacred circle, with a greater energy pull than even Stonehenge: "in the days before we had Christianity, people used to pray in that circle. That's an old kind of kirk, that's all it is." (12)

It is through Ina and Catriona MacEochan, the island's medical doctor, that Lizzie meets Maria Milleny, "the Daft Artist on the Far West End." (13) and here the second story begins to take shape—Maria's story.

It is in Maria's story that the reader learns how Maria came to Cailleach. She had exhibited a set of her paintings called "Lives of the Saints" in a London gallery, "a . . . favourite of the Pretty People." (21) One of the viewers was Catriona MacEochan, an old school chum of the owner. Catriona attended the show because her childhood friend had told her that the paintings were not what one would expect from such a title: the paintings were feminist revisionist interpretations of selected saint's lives. Catriona buys the Saint Bridget painting with the monograph: "On a moonlit shore in a cold northern landscape, the saint strokes the arched neck of a blue-grey swan who has come to light on the edge of a turbulent sea." (23) She is drawn to the painting like the cows to the Ring because the background and landscape are authentic representations of Cailleach. When Maria admits not ever having been to Cailleach, though she has captured the light and landscape "exactly," Catriona invites her to the island and to her castle, fare paid, to deliver the painting. True, Maria has never been to

Cailleach; however, her mother was born and raised on the island. Thus her ability to draw background and landscapes "exactly" is not due to the psychic ability assumed by Catriona; she has seen photos.

Maria does not deliver the painting, but two years later she decides to visit Cailleach. She is jobless and broke and depressed and creatively sterile. Visiting a place that is described as having "the harshest climate in the west of Scotland and a form of Christianity that matches it," (26) fits her mood and her state in life. A guidebook calls it "a Protestant island, where 'fornication is a mere peccadillo, compared to idleness.'" (57)

Although one of Maria's motives in journeying to Cailleach is to view her mother's home land, it is not her primary motive. Motive comes from an unnamed desire to quell the feelings of restlessness and uprootedness that overtook her after she finished the show titled "Lives of the Saints."

As Galford brings Maria to Cailleach and the home of Catriona, Cailleach itself (herself) becomes both place and character, where, as Catriona tells Maria "her hills have eyes and her breezes carry gossip," (35) and where stones draw beasts towards them. Catriona shows Maria that attachment to place goes far deeper than feeling comfortable in a house on a piece of land that allows one to live securely. It shows that land is a living being, interacting with other living beings. That "being" may not speak English—or Gaelic—but speak it does: her hills have eyes and her breezes carry gossip. The land, and the trees, and the birds in the air, and the tides of the sea communicate to the islanders who relate to Cailleach as a living being, not as inert background.

Not only do Cailleach's "hills have eyes and her breezes carry gossip," adds Catriona, "there isn't a bird flying overhead but is in my pay," (35) giving Maria an indication that Catriona's influence on the island is more than medical and historical. Indeed, Catriona, though an M.D., is also an ardent and seasoned practitioner of the occult.

Enter another character: Dr. Stephanie Stonebridge, Stoney to her friends. Dr. Stonebridge is "a small, dark woman, skinny as a ten-year-old boy." (35) She is an archaeologist leading a group interested not in the Ring but in the garden of the nunnery of Bride/Saint Bridget, "to see what the old girls grew and how they grew it." (36)

On a sight-seeing tour of the island, Catriona introduces Maria to "a large, rambling ruin," the convent of Bride, built around the tenth century, where the archaeologists have been digging. Bride's story begins to unfold at the site of the convent. It is important that Bride's story begins to be heard, because it forms the heart for the other three stories to build on and around.

When Maria suggests that the Celtic goddess Bride was a saint, known to the Irish as Saint Bridget, Catriona's reply is, "That, my dear, was much later. And merely an aberration." (50) Catriona, then, aligns herself with the history of goddess consciousness.[27]

On the other hand, the writer of the spiritual history of the island who writes that "the ungrateful lot who live there light their fires for . . . Bride," was under the influence of the *Christian* founding fathers' notion of Bride. From the perspective of the goddess-conscious islanders (as opposed to the writer of those islanders' history) that statement is not only inaccurate, it is written from ignorance: when the islanders light their fires, they light them for *two* goddesses—Bride *and* Cailleach. Those, then, who truly understand the history of Cailleach as both island/woman and Bride as a goddess/woman would not call the present-day islanders an "ungrateful lot."

Catriona is the one to tell Maria (and the reader) that "Bride belongs to Cailleach. And Cailleach belongs to her." (48) That before the convent, there was a temple. That a long time ago there were a lot of hasty burials, "done . . . by clumsy hands," (49). It is at this time that Maria has her first vision of what happened: the knock on the door, "the glint of red-gold beards before the club thumps down," the invasion, the slaughtering, and the moment when the "Fire itself finally goes out, when a crouching bundle of rags rises up from a dark corner, and pushes the last invader into it." (49) Maria's journey to "retrieve what has been lost," has begun.

Maria's journey into the cratered night is not a straight path across the landscape of her memory. It resembles a labyrinth with its maze of twists and turns. For the first three months on Cailleach, she lacks any desire to paint, draw, or sculpt; her time is taken up with walks to the pre-historical sites or with books on medieval island history; her loss of Self is so evident that, "She gives up looking in mirrors. Just as well. She isn't there any more." (93)

What begins as a desire to give herself time to find her motivation to create again turns into an escape into non-being as well as non-doing. Even when Catriona gives Maria a large and well-stocked supply of paints, canvases, and wooden stretchers as a winter solstice present, it does not entice Maria to begin to paint again.

An action by Catriona, however, moves Maria and her journey off of the plateau where she was stuck: Catriona takes Maria and her belongings in her land rover to a small, white-washed cottage that she owns on the far west side of the island. (Catriona's castle is on the northeast side.) It is in this cottage, on the far west side of the island, that Maria hears "the Atlantic smash itself against the shore. Until the rhythms of her dreams, and the flow of her blood, synchronize with the ocean tides, Maria sleeps very badly." (105)

She walks the beach every night, "to look at the light." (105) (In the nights of early summer, darkness lasts only an hour or two). One night she thinks she sees the seaweed-gatherer, "riding the waves into shore . . . at second glance, . . . vanished, leaving only a faint tingling along Maria's spine as proof of her passage." (106) Maria's Self has moved from her plateau and is spiraling farther into the cratered night. Retrieval of "what's been lost" is about to begin. "What's been lost" is the story within the story within the story. This inner-chambered story takes on clarity and insight as Maria settles into the isolation of the cottage and a mediating, third-person narrator unveils, unlayers and discloses the life of Mhairi to the reader.

Mhairi is a tenth or eleventh-century nun in the convent of Saint Bride, during a time when Bride changed from goddess to saint, from Bride to Bridget. Mhairi became a nun because, as a female, her other choice in life was to marry a man selected by her father to bind territories. This man, a loathsome man, had already buried three wives and was more than three times her age. She was fourteen when the choice of nunnery or marriage was put before her.

In the convent, Mhairi is taught "the mystery of making books with words and pictures in them. It may take you twenty years, if we are spared and if the Fire stays alight . . . but you will be able to make things that will last longer than any of us" says Sister Bloduedd to Mhairi. (111–12) For a year she learns to shape letters; for five years she copies a story, a disturbing story, but she copies what comes from Bloduedd's lips. She learns to make colors for the pictures in the story using wildflowers, seaweeds, shells, pebbles, "seventeen different shades of blue," (112) red from berries, russet-brown from menstrual blood, "carefully collected and dried out in earthenware basins near the Fire," (113) silver and gold from locked boxes. (113)

The Sisters possess the *Book of Bride* that they read aloud, in a group, once a year on the summer solstice, "that night in the year when the light never quite disappears." (115) However, "every year, the words change slightly. Even if the same reader, in the same sequence, takes the same passages, year after year, it happens" (116)—except for certain immutables: "the fruitbearing tree, the linked spirals, the gaily striped snake nibbling its own tail . . . and the sow with seven piglets." (116)

What is the *Book of Bride?* It is a Gospel, a Gospel about Mary birthing twins. According to the story, she bore Jesus and she bore a female who was secreted away by the midwife assisting Mary at her birthing time. Since female babies were sold or given away or exchanged for food or shelter, no one paid any attention to the female twin, or to the midwife: "And by the time her twin brother was nailed on the cross, . . . she was long forgotten." (116) This is the story, told with much detail and embellished with pictures of foxes, weasels, snakes and dragons, that takes Mhairi years and years to produce.

While she writes and draws, one of the nuns during one of those years discovers a cellar beneath the garden. (She fell through the earth into the sub cellar while digging in the garden). In it are two perfect skeletons of women. On the walls are pictures scratched into the surface: "a . . . tree bearing dangling globes of fruit, a striped snake swallowing itself, some spirals interlinked . . . a snouted beast suckling seven smaller ones." And in the floor of earth, a pit for a fire. (117) This discovery means that the women who died in the cellar lived when Bride was a goddess and the convent was a temple. It would be a time well before the Christian era, when belief in goddess consciousness and cosmic forces prevailed among the people.

The Sisters of Bride in the Christian era were not a stationary group. They could not be. Sometimes elements such as floods forced them out; sometimes the Catholic Celtic bishops; sometimes the Roman papacy. They were, then, nomadic. Building on a site where the followers of the goddess Bride had built would not have been unusual, and according to the Reverend Mother, not coincidental: "this place was chosen for a reason. Most annoyingly, the chronicler never thought to mention what it was." (117)

The Celtic Church fathers needed to control the Sisters of Saint Bride because they could read and write and thus were dangerous to the priests. These priests come upon a plan to extinguish Saint Bride's Fire, "their quaint little sacred flame. Old pagan relic." (121) Extinguishing the Fire would extinguish the driving force behind the energy and intelligence of the Sisters as well as bring them under total control of Rome. (121)[28]

The Sisters do not give in easily; indeed, it takes even more than the murder of the Reverend Mother and the appointment of her killer as Abbess to subdue them. Bloduedd and Mhairi work ever more feverishly to finish the manuscripts, as edicts such as: "all trees, stones, and fires, formerly the objects of pagan worship, are now decreed to be anathema," and "the Brothers . . . of North Uist and Iona . . . will mak[e] the illuminated books. . . . The scriptorium Sisters will be redeployed to the sewing brigade" are levied against them. (125)[29]

Forced to stop their writing after completing two manuscripts of the Book, Mhairi breaks one of the numerous rules set down since the new abbess arrived: she leaves the convent for a short while to visit her younger sister who had no choice but to marry the man Mhairi refused. The younger sister, bitter but alive, does consent to do Mhairi a favor: she hides one of the manuscripts that Mhairi secrets out of the convent in her house. "'Keep it very, very secret,' Mhairi requests. 'And keep it safe. And if I don't come back for it and time goes on, and the bump in your belly proves to be a daughter, ask her to do the same. And for Bride's sake, don't ever tell anyone. Especially not your husband.'" (129–30)

All other copies of the Book are found and destroyed through burning. As punishment for breaking the rules, Mhairi is confined to the earth cellar underneath the kitchen garden, the same cellar where the other two women's skeletons were found. Into her nun's habit she has sewn some pages of an unfinished copy of the manuscript. While passing the time, she draws spirals and snakes and sows on the walls. But then she hears far-away sounds that disturb and puzzle her—"faint screams, roars, splintering wood, clanging metal." (131)

This is the vision that Maria had when she first looked down on the convent of Saint Bride with Catriona. It was a vision of the rape and slaughter of the nuns in the convent by a tribe of Vikings in about the eleventh century. Mhairi would not know it, but she would die as the last of the "Fire-women" (131)—all the others killed by the Vikings—and she would be found, nearly a thousand years later, by Dr. Stonebridge and Maria, in the earth cellar in the convent garden, sitting against the wall.

Back in the late twentieth century, Maria, on the far west side of the island, is being battered around the beach by an Arctic storm that the islanders call "the whips of Saint Columba." It "slams in from the place where the old mapmakers put their sea monsters. . . . And it goes on for a long, long time." (135) To avoid a serious case of cabin fever, Maria battles the wind for control of her door, temporarily wins and walks the shore until she is "scoured clean as a pebble . . . grounded." (135) The energy from the storm's wind works as a positive force to remove the psychic debris from her spirit that has prevented her from being able to paint. Returning to her cottage, she sees she is not alone: "Someone has kept the fire going in her absence. . . . It's the sea-weed-woman." (136)

The only other time the seaweed-woman has been mentioned thus far is when Maria sees the woman collecting seaweed from the beach after another storm. As readers, we have no idea who she is or why she was even alluded to in Maria's moment of frustration, even though the narrative is half-finished. Except for the clue in *the*. The allusion was not to *a* seaweed-woman, but *the* seaweed-woman. Is she a guardian angel? A fairy godmother? If so, she neither looks nor acts like one: "Maria's visitor is as waterlogged as she is, and her sodden, shapeless clothes steam slightly from the fire's warmth." (136) Galford puts us in the mind and eyes of Maria as together, we try to figure out who this woman is and why she is where she is. In true reader-response fashion, reader and text mutually interact in a conversational dance.

A clue comes quickly: "the seaweed-woman's face is identical to her own." (136) Reader and Maria have entered another layer of reality here. As Maria "pretends everything's ordinary, she says, 'I've seen you before, you know. Gathering seaweed. Is it for the processing plant?'" (136)

The woman is at least flesh—we are uncertain of "blood"—because, when Maria touches the woman's arm, "the flesh is as clammy and goose-bumped as Maria's own." (137) Maria uses the excuse that it is normal to encounter a centuries-old woman "in the flesh" with "I do have Celtic blood. Perhaps we're nineteenth cousins, a thousand times removed." (137) In her flip, off-beat response, afraid to confront the terror that awaits her in that cratered night of female memory—the terror of knowing/the terror of not knowing— Maria, nonetheless, has moved a few paces farther into that memory to retrieve what has been lost. She decides that she must know.

They are indeed ancestors; Maria is not so much a distant cousin of the seaweed-woman as a reincarnation. Maria tries conversing with her visitor, telling her of the time she had seen her picking up seaweed and floating across the water, (138) but the conversation goes nowhere because the woman speaks only Gaelic. The woman points to herself and "says something that sounds like 'Varri'" (138)—a name very close to "Mhairi." The woman offers Maria some bread she is carrying; Maria, "expecting it to be hard and stale as old bones" discovers that it is "sweet and yeasty" with "a faint iodine sharpness, a spicing of seaweed." (139)

The woman stays the night with Maria in her bed, and "her [the seaweed-woman's] lips, fingers, and everything they touch glow in the darkness. Mirror-images, copperspeckled moonstones, flow together."(139)

In the morning, Maria is alone, no trace or odor of the seaweed-woman. Dressing and going out to the beach—the storm has passed—"she buries her face in a clump of gleaming blue-black seaweed." (140) Either she is "gey strange" as one of the sheepherders says to himself when he sees her, or Maria is ready to "retrieve what is lost . . . in the female memory" . . . or both.

If spirits are going to visit Maria in Cailleach, a seaweed-woman-spirit would be an understandable visitor. Seaweed is, indeed, a product of the ocean; it is a product that has healing properties because it carries elements of the ocean in its form, the same elements that we humans carry in our blood, the same elements that surrounded us in the amniotic waters in our mother's womb.[30] So consciously or unconsciously, we all are pulled to the sea and the weeds it produces by our blood-and-water ties. Living, literally, on the shore of the sea, Maria's pull to the weeds would be even stronger.

What effect does the night visitor have on Maria other than creating the urge in her to bury her face in a clump of weeds? She starts to paint again in order "to sort out her messy life." (140) She finds that she has sold some paintings in London from her "Lives of the Saints" group, so she quits living off of Catriona (as Maria perceives it, she is "living off of" her friend; Catriona does not perceive it that way), and starts to pay for her own groceries. Till this time, Catriona has given her the cottage rent-free and paid for her food. Next, she acquires a job pumping gas at the one and only gas station on the island in order to further release herself from her financial ties to Catriona.

Then she paints. After close to a year's absence from the canvas, she paints. Her creativity begins to bloom as the year's dormancy takes root and flowers. Her paintings are mythic in theme, but the subject is the same on all of the canvases: Catriona MacEochan. Maria paints Catriona as a "witch dropping snakes and froglets into a bubbling cauldron; as Mary Queen of Scots bravely approaching the headsman's block, attempting to commune with the Other Side, playing her planchette like a tiny piano; a stone carved fertility goddess all mountainous bosom," and others. (141) When Catriona comes to Maria's cottage to view them, she sees them for what they are, "a pouring out of bile" so that Maria can now do "serious work," (143) and she is not offended. Maria is now ready to plunge into the cratered night.

The serious work begins at the garage/gas station, where Maria has made a bargain with the owner. As long as she performs her duties of waiting on customers and pumping gas, she can have any and all of the three mountains of scrap-metal behind the garage as well as access to the garage work space and welding equipment. Here "tall, tortured, semi-human shapes come unbidden out of her blowtorch." (145) Maria now takes giant strides into female memory where she is not only "retrieving what's been lost," she is beginning to "reconceive" and shortly will "give birth."

Her next visit from the seaweed-woman comes in a dream. In it, the seaweed-woman is unrolling a scroll with "edges of a richly-coloured, gilded illumination." (150) The reader knows that the scroll of Mhairi fits this description. As of yet, Maria has no understanding, historical or ancestral, of Mhairi. Only the reader and the narrator know of her; instead of journeying with Maria to come to know the seaweed-woman as Self, we watch Maria take her journey, knowing what she will encounter if she allows herself the openness to whatever lies in her future, an openness that brings not only joy but pain.

As Maria searches to pull more information from the last brief dream with the seaweed-woman, she works on a labor-intensive project that lasts for thirty days and thirty nights: "Women's faces, none of them known to her, swim up out of her dreams. They pique and plague her until she finds some way to reproduce them." (157) She does indeed find "some way," in the workshop of the garage.

As she works, "she overhears . . . scraps of conversation, . . . tastes strong broth . . . smells warms wool and sweat and menstrual blood (not her own) . . . coarse cloth lies heavy on her shoulders . . . and sometimes . . . she is tripped up by an invisible hem around her ankles." (157)

What has she created in those thirty days and thirty nights? Nuns. "Made out of scrap metal and fourteen feet tall." (158) Maria puts these nuns back on the convent site of their protectress Saint Bride, where they have been absent since the eleventh century when they were poisoned, starved, and killed outright by priests, an abbess and a horde of Viking raiders searching for booty. (49, 83, 84)

Dr. Stonebridge is the first to find them as she arrives at the digging site earlier than the rest of her crew. She "laughs until tears run." (158)

The Rev. Murdo MacNeish, upholder of the Christian religion on the island, has a different reaction since the statues represent to him "another little slide down the slippery slope towards the worship of graven images." (158) Not to worry, says Maria. He is not convinced. Maria is right, of course. It is not that they are "graven images" that will draw people, even from Sweden, to Cailleach to view these sculptures as well as the many others Maria has "reconceive[d] and give[n] birth to"; it is Maria's talent as an artist that draws them. What no one in the story realizes yet, including Maria, is that the sculptures are worth viewing because Maria is sculpting from her self rooted to Self, her female memory, her ancestry. And having found her way to the center of this labyrinth, she is on her way to finding the wholeness that she came to seek when she journeyed to Cailleach almost two years ago.

Catriona comes in and out of Maria's life, sometimes as a friend, sometimes as a gadfly, sometimes as an intruder, at least according to Maria. However Maria sees her, it is Catriona who has noticed in Maria's work in London the spark of a spirit struggling to find her Being expressed through her art. And it was Catriona's generous financial offer that is a motivating force for Maria to visit Cailleach, for finding one's Being in artistic expression needs uninterrupted time and a room of one's own, freed from the necessity of having to earn enough money to buy food, clothing, and shelter, as well as supplies for one's artistic medium of choice. Thus, a patron or an essential angel is necessary, no matter the personality.

Maria has some difficulty taking Catriona's offer on face value: "What's the catch?" For Catriona, there is no catch; besides being a pagan M.D., she is "on first name terms with all the island's ghosts." (11) That is why she freely offers financial assistance to Maria, with no strings. Having viewed her show in the London art gallery, Catriona knows that Maria has the ability to bring Bride back "home" to Cailleach and rekindle her sacred Fire. Ironically, it will be Catriona who rekindles that Fire; rekindling the Fire will be the arc that sparks Maria's opportunity to bring Bride back home.

Besides, Catriona knows what "poor" means. When Catriona first went to Edinburgh to medical school, she went as a disinherited daughter. Her twentieth-century father gives forth with a tenth-century edict by demanding that she marry someone who would bind two vast land holdings. She said no. He excluded her from the family, but not from the will. She paid her way through college by fortunetelling, reading palms and ouija boards, scrying crystals and drawing pentagrams; she was a speywife, and a successful one, performing her rituals under the name of Madame Brigantia, a medieval name for Bride. When she inherited the castle after her father's death, (Catriona is an only child), she inherited tomes on the occult, some of them dating back to the twelfth century.

Anyone who sincerely follows the powers of the occult knows that what one does not do frivolously is to place hexes on others, because the hex returns threefold to the sender. The same holds true for helping another person. If, in her helping Maria financially find her path to create what was most important to her, Catriona put strings on that call to help, the powers would undo something in Catriona's life threefold. Being sincere in helping Maria, Catriona could only benefit.[31]

Before Maria can bring Bride back home, the owner of the garage/gas station sells his shop to a Scotsman who will turn the garage into a small factory. In a lavish farewell gesture, the shop owner gives Maria whatever she can haul away, which is everything she had been working with: the mountains of scrap metal and the welding equipment. However, Maria is now without a regular paycheck, meager though it was.

The new owner, Scotty McCrumb, a scurrilous relative of Catriona, intends to "make Good" in Cailleach as he has in America, Taiwan, the Philippines and Glasgow by selling tacky souvenirs exported around the world: bears in kilts, Loch Ness monsters made of tartan plaid, socks knitted with the map of Scotland on the sides. Maria signs on as the part-time art designer. His hired help: island housewives who want a little extra cash and something to do, says Scotty in his best paternalistic voice. His factories around the world are all staffed with housewives. What he does not count on is the fact that these women from Cailleach are as subversive as they are intelligent.

Like the English women in the stories narrated by Rozsika Parker in *The Subversive Stitch* who used needlework to subvert attempts by the dominant culture to keep them oppressed, the Cailleach women, with Maria as their leader, subvert Scotty's philosophy with needlework to spread the "real truth" about the happenings on the Outer Hebrides: on the tea towels, the Scottish unemployment statistics; on the ashtrays, Scottish lung-cancer death rates; on the coffee mugs, the names and death dates of Highland women burned as witches; on the shortbread tins, a map of the NATO bases and American nuclear missile sites, and hand-knitted baby seals and whales wearing "SAVE US" badges. (183–84)

Though Scotty's fury at Maria can be heard across the island, his profits continue to rise. However, his grant money runs out and he leaves the islanders in a precarious position: though the dead-end economy on Cailleach has picked up, closing the factory will tumble them downwards to their usually low employment rates. That means that alcohol consumption will begin to rise again, and with it, a rise in spousal abuse. Ellen Galford sends Scotty back to America and leaves us in suspense as to what will happen to the island's economy because more important things are happening.

One evening in the castle, Maria listens to Catriona as she tells
her about the castle ghost's visit. One thing that has disturbed
Catriona is that she could cast no spell to make the ghost stay: "I
tried a spell I know—for holding them—but she slipped away. And
neither the [ouija] board nor the pentagram nor the candles nor
the words of power will bring her back." (181) This ghost, however,
has left a trace of her presence, "an odd sort of iodine smell." (181)
The seaweed-woman visits more women than Maria.

Maria, having become obsessed with the seaweed-woman,
tries to find her again by visiting the Cailleach Ring; at midnight,
she goes to a particular stone, "reaches out her hand and probes
until she finds the spiral deeply etched into its surface. . . . She
presses her face into a smooth hollow . . . and whispers into the
stone: 'Where is she?'" (182) What Maria has forgotten is that the
seaweed-woman's face is her face. In her compulsion to "get to the
bottom of this," she leaves the sacred space of her Self to enter the
profane space of jealousy toward Catriona. That action undermines
the progress she has made on her journey toward retrieval and
reconception. She herself is unaware that she truly can trust
Catriona. "Then she listens. A low, low humming . . . a sense of
warmth. . . . But no other signals." (182)

Even though she asks the stone, "Where is she?", when a different reincarnation of the seaweed-woman presents herself to
Maria a few weeks later, she is totally unprepared for it. For a while
Maria was open to Earth's call, but her jealousy toward Catriona
deafened her to answers to her question.

Stoney and her students find the cellar that contains the
skeleton of Mhairi. Like the nun who lived in Saint Bride's convent
back in the tenth or eleventh century and fell through a spot in the
garden to uncover the women's skeletons in the cellar, so too the
students, in their digging, find the cellar by falling into it; in it, a
woman's skeleton. Upon seeing the skeleton (Stoney brings Maria
to the discovery), "her [Maria's] mouth is filled with the piercing,
briny taste and smell of seaweed; her lips are salty." (195) She clam-

bers up the ladder and out into the morning air; for what Maria sees "in her mind's eye," sitting upright, leaning against the chamber wall, "the face fleshed out into something recognizable, the reddish strands that lay limply along the polished skull," (195) is, as with the seaweed-woman, her own face. She is aware that her face and the skeleton's face are identical. She is unaware that the skeleton is Mhairi's, the nun sentenced to the cellar by the abbess who took over the convent of Saint Bride for the Isle bishop and was left to die when the Vikings came and killed all the others.

The experience causes Maria to fear sleep, for when she sleeps, she dreams. The next night, after trying unsuccessfully to stay awake by working on some sketches, she does fall asleep at her table and is awakened by "the sense of a shadow" passing her cottage window. She opens the door. No one is there: "the tide is high but the iodine smell . . . is overpowering." (197) Earth is calling loudly and clearly to Maria, but she still cannot quite fit the pieces together that are before her to create that wholeness. Something is still missing.

It is Catriona (through working her planchette) who revs up the tension and conflict over the new discoveries by proposing to the Rev. MacNeish at the Community Council meeting that it is possible "'that Christianity as we know it might be based on a typographical error. . . . With a mere change of a couple of letters in the original text,' she continues brightly 'the Son of God could, in actuality, have been a daughter . . . there may have been a female trinity: the Triple Goddess . . . The boy . . . just a decoy to distract the Emperor's secret police.'" (198)

Catriona knows that Stoney has also found some pages of the *Book of Bride* in a special iron box along with Mhairi's skeleton. On those pages is part of the story of Bride's role in Jesus's birth: some of the lettering and artwork still readable, the colors still bright and clear.

The story that can be read from the saved pages is that Mary birthed twins and the saint/goddess-midwife spirited away the girl, the afterbirth, and the bloodied clothing. The midwife was Bride. As the one and only Reverend who upholds Christianity on the island, Murdo MacNeish's opinion of that idea as, "Rubbish and blasphemous balderdash." (198)

Catriona lights the Fire extinguished for ten centuries by drawing attention to Stoney's discovery, as she will reveal *her* discovery, whose consequences will fan that flame to light up the skies over Cailleach. Buried in the walls of Catriona's castle is the one extant copy of the *Book of Bride* that Mhairi secreted out of the convent to her sister. "It has always been in my family," Catriona tells Maria when Maria asks where she got it. Catriona can trace her ancestry back to a male consort of King James Stuart. The MacEochan clan owned the entire island of Cailleach at one time because King James deeded it to this man, her father's, and Catriona's, male ancestor. Ten centuries after Mhairi's sister had kept the *Book* safe, it came to rest in the MacEochan castle. It turned up again one night when a storm tore the pipes off the eastern wall of the castle a month or so before Stoney found the corpse, about the time the seaweed-woman visited Catriona. Though some of the stones holding it in were damaged, the book was intact.

After teasing the Reverend with pieces of information about Christian history, and after allowing Maria to examine the entire volume, Catriona takes it to Edinburgh to "Tell the World." (206) The secrecy surrounding Bride, the Nativity, and Christian history vanishes as Catriona decides that the price for this secrecy has been too high already. The Christian patriarchy may not have become so entrenched for so many centuries had this particular secret been revealed at an earlier time.

Selling the book so that "the World" can participate in her discovery is the first step; using some of the money to buy Scotty's factory and turn it into a workers' cooperative is the second. Not only will the island's economy remain steady, the employed women will own and operate the factory with no paternalistic boss or absentee landlord to make rules and quotas.

How does Maria fit into this background? Seeing, touching, smelling, even imaging the ambiance that helped Mhairi recreate the *Book of Bride* has nudged Maria farther along her journey; this time, however, she is on the way out of the labyrinth. The very innermost spot of Maria's labyrinth, the place where there is utter darkness and utter silence, where all sense of time and space is turned around, where the worms work and the roots grow, (some call it the womb of the Mother,) is where she sees her face on the skeleton of the nun: "she finds herself on the far west side, in front of her cottage, with no sense of the time that has passed or the distance she has covered. "She . . . turns towards the beach, and walks down to meet the advancing tide. She stands on the shore until the icy water grips her ankles, then lets out a long, loud banshee howl in a voice that belongs to someone else." (197)

In finding her historical ancestry, she finds her female ancestral memory; with that discovery, she finds the pieces to the picture that give it wholeness. In finding those historical pieces, order forms from chaos and self roots to Self. In finding Self she has found her power, both personal and artistic, power gleaned as "insight and grounding."[32] She has come through to healing. When Maria's understanding of her ancestry becomes clear, a change comes over her and she is able to transfer the clear-flowing energy of her spirit into the creation of her scrap metal sculptures that hold meaning, now, for *her* life.

Maria also discovers that she does not need visits from the seaweed-woman to make connection, to create, "to give birth." Her first creation after this discovery? ". . . a faceless woman . . . her streaming hair in a tangle of metal seaweed, and she carries a basket filled with polished stones." (209) Maria places her creation outside the cottage. "'What's her name?' asks Catriona. . . . 'The Walker on the Beach'" answers Maria. (209)

The title is ambiguous enough to satisfy the curious. But Maria knows that this Walker could also be called "the Seaweed-Woman" or even "Cailleach": goddess, crone, wise woman, island. As a goddess, Cailleach has the ability to carry massive stones in her apron, or her creeling basket, to the sacred sites to build the sacred circles. (211)[33] She shows the light and the dark side of womanhood: when she is friendly, "she's the good Old Woman"; when she feels stormy, "she's the Queen of Stones." (211) Maria recreated Cailleach's image, adding the particular touch of streaming hair that "is a tangle of metal seaweed."

While at the cottage, Catriona confides to Maria that she is feeling depressed over selling the *Book*, fearing that when she sold it for a price in the world of commodities, Bride left the island. It is now Maria's turn to console Catriona. "'She's still here. Promise.' says Maria. . . . 'Trust me. And watch this space.'" (210) Maria has a different point of view as to what keeps Bride on Cailleach as a living spirit.

What does Maria know about Bride, goddess and saint? What did the nuns know that made them protect her and her sacred Fire to the death? Bride was the major Celtic triple goddess, "the primordial Celtic Great Mother herself,"[34] a Celtic Triple Goddess including the maiden, mother, and crone of the lunar cycle: maiden to the waxing moon; mother to the full moon; crone to the waning moon. She was goddess of fire, healers, smithcraft (ironwork in particular), childbirth, poets, among others. The Irish consider her goddess legend as having great importance; when Christianity became the dominant religion, the priests, with Machiavellian astuteness, did not turn her into a devil or sinful woman but into Saint Bridgit. As part of its strategy to convert the pagans, the Catholic Church kept her pagan feast day for her saint's day: February 1. In Ireland, traditionally, February 1 is the first day of spring.

It is said that when Bride was born, fire surrounded her head; it is also said that she was Mary's midwife. Images associated with her are the serpent, the cow, the sow, the horse, fire, the sun (a sun goddess), milk, and wells. She was compassionate, protective and generous. She was also a weaver and a needleworker. She is a goddess who cannot be banished from dreams, try as some have to do so; she has survived all onslaughts.

The Fire is important because as long as it burns, Bride is present. The Fire was quenched in the tenth to the twelfth centuries, depending on the citation one reads. Thus, when Catriona finds the *Book* it is a sign to many that Bride is still on the island, even though her Fire has been quenched for centuries.[35]

To manifest Bride's spirit in material form, Maria's first display resembles the stones that make up the Cailleach Ring. However, the "stones" are made of aluminum, a mixture of ancient and contemporary images: portraits "of anonymous nuns, of . . . Ina Isbister, of Catriona with a dangling stethoscope and a high-pointed witch's hat, . . . a blue-eyed Viking maiden . . . island women. . . . They brood all together over a . . . slab-like altar . . . [where] trussed up, lies a black-clad figure in clerical collar." (211). The cleric is obviously Rev. MacNeish, "sporting a pair of bushy eyebrows that have been deftly built up from layers of flaking rust." (211) Maria calls it "Stone Circle II."

The season of the year is late November. Maria continues to create, but Bride herself has not appeared, and she will not appear until the eve of Hogmanay, the Scottish recognition of the New Year. On the eve of the New Year, there is always a bonfire next to Catriona's castle, always an icy, cutting wind, always entertainment by Snorri's Marauders who use Catriona's library to set up their equipment, usually rain, always coffee laced with whiskey, always vats of Catriona's vegetable soup, with garlic, simmering in cauldrons in sheds temporarily erected for the evening, always "gossip around the flames." (216) Only two duties ever keep any of the islanders from participating in this ceremony: attending a birth, or death.

Five minutes before midnight, all are assembled, well fed, thirst slacked and duly entertained, and Maria removes the covering from her sculpture which is situated at the far end of the beach from the castle and bonfire.

Imperfectly illuminated by the bonfire, a massive moon-round, smiling female face beams out from an aureole of gold and silver and copper sun-bursts. She is a carnival giantess, of painted metal, with vast piratical hooped earrings dangling from someplace within her crown of metallic curls . . . called "The Queen of the Fire." (217) This "Queen of the Fire" is Bride.

A spectacular way to begin a new year; nonetheless, the Reverend MacNeish thunders through the crowd proclaiming, "that is a graven image to end all graven images. . . . Have you [all] forfeited your places among the Lord's Elect?" (218) Try as he may, here and in his sermons, no one on the island really pays much attention to the Reverend, even when he and Catriona have a go-round in front of the queen and the fire in a scene that is reminiscent of Merlin, Arthur's wizard, and one of Britain's female witches vying for the honor of High Wizard. There is shape-changing, cursing, and summoning. As they are both drenched from the rain's downpour, Catriona "offers him a bowl of soup in her castle. He declines." (220)

At home, on New Year's Day, having breakfast with his family, the Reverend dies, choking on a bone of the kipper he is eating while reading the *Sunday Sentinel*, "which has arrived on the Monday night ferry." (220) The choking and dying have been brought on by a blinding insight the Reverend gained while reading an article on Maria headlined, "Island Storm Over Blasphemous Art." (221) It seems that Maria is a niece to the Reverend.

Maria's mother had been born and raised on Cailleach. At seventeen she left the island because she was banned from the family for having become engaged to marry an Irish Catholic from Dublin. She and her husband, John Milleny, moved to Australia, never returning to either Cailleach or Ireland. She and the Reverend were brother and sister. Though Maria knew that her mother was from Cailleach, she did not know that the Reverend was her uncle. Nor would it have bothered her. Her uncle, on the other hand, was so bothered that, "He stabs a piece of kipper viciously, and chokes on it." (222)

Thus when Maria leaves London, she is not escaping the hotbed of artistic enterprise and networking in Britain, to live for a bit on the outermost island of the Outer Hebrides, an island " so distant . . . so difficult of access, that few tourists will take the trouble to visit its clutch of antiquities." (26) Instead, she is trying to face that part of her that felt split, restless, uprooted, creatively sterile. Accepting support from Catriona is a way to help her begin her journey toward healing.

Like any of us who begin such a journey, we never know the full impact of what truly lies ahead. If we did, there would be no need to make the journey, the physical one or the inward one. But being willing to make it gives Maria hope that her female creative Self can be found and her healing to wholeness be realized. For the Reverend, knowledge brings death; for Maria, knowledge gives birth to the Self, as it comes through the "cratered night of female memory."

This story is about Bride, Mhairi, Maria and Catriona. It is also about Lizzie, who drives (then ferries) to Cailleach to do a story on Maria. As the story closes, Lizzie's boss has canned her script for the film on Maria and ordered Lizzie to Portugal to cover the World Cup in soccer. Lizzie quits her job in disgust. The narrative ends on Lizzie's story as Maria offers Lizzie room in her little cottage and a table to write on so that she can turn the film into a book. (229) Lizzie accepts. It is the end of the book, but not the end of projec tions about the characters.

A feminist reader-response reader realizes that Maria makes the same offer to Lizzie that Catriona offered Maria, and that is important to realize. Here, modest circumstances notwithstanding, Maria continues a tradition set forth in a time labeled as pre-biblical or pre-patriarchal when human life existed in a symbiotic relationship with Earth in order to continue the cycle of birth, life, death, rebirth.[36] That symbiotic bond was broken in historical time, and spirit was divorced from matter, self divorced from Self.

Virginia Woolf was not allowed to walk the paths that the dons at Oxford walked because she was female. That she came from a family with money to provide her with her own room and no need to labor for survival in order to write helped immeasurably, but one of the strings attached to her for the provisions was her swearing to secrecy for the sexual abuse she endured by those same family members who provided her with the time and the space.

By the late 1980s Galford's Maria, Lizzie and Catriona can live outside that historical, patriarchal system that bound Virginia Woolf so tightly that it silenced her by suicide, that pushed Dulcie to kill, that forced Gertie and Mrs. Anderson to give up their creative callings. Maria can pass the offer of space and time on to Lizzie because Catriona has given to Maria the time and space to create, with no strings. Paradoxically, however, Catriona is able to act in this way because she inherited a great deal of money and property from her father, there being no brothers to receive it. An offer without strings is an offer of love. Thus Catriona is a healer in a much broader sense than merely being an M.D., because, through a gesture of love, she gives Maria the time and space to enter the cratered night of female memory. It takes time to go back tens of thousands of years in memory. Without that offer, rooting self to Self is not possible at all. No offer, no experience. No experience, no chance to root and heal.

In turn, Maria continues the tradition to offering time, space, and food to another female artist who cannot create *without* the offer, giving continuity to the vital act of co-creation meted out those tens of thousands of years ago in a context of hope for the continuum, broken in historical time by the creation of the patriarchy. In turn, Maria's offer to Lizzie is an offer made from love. "Make it into a book. You can stay with me as long as you like. I even have a table you can write on." Lizzie reflects, "I know this fantastic offer will not be repeated. So I do." (229) Bride still lives.

Galford, then, takes the story of Lizzie, who is writing a film script, and brings that story full circle by linking Lizzie not only to Maria but to Galford herself as writer of a book about Bride. The spirals of writer and story, painter and sculptor, healer and witch, pagan and Christian, goddess and saint, roots and Self, fire and spirit, circle endlessly and forever. A continuum.

There are many paths to heal one's Self/spirit. Many women writers have found that, by becoming revisionist writers, "revising the male Maker's texts" and "shattering the mirror that has so long reflected what every woman was supposed to be,"[37] they have created in their writing a spiritual quality that leads them on a path to healing cultural contradictions about women.

The same can be said for Ellen Galford. In writing a woman-centered narrative, Galford "shatter[s] the mirror." In creating Maria, who through sculpture finds her ancestral roots and thus her healing, Galford has successfully layered character and narrative so that the context, the texture, the fabric of the story tells me that this is "a story that's true."

A weave of women in Send My Roots Rain
by Ibis Gómez-Vega

I was first drawn to Ibis Gómez-Vega's novel because I recognized the title as a line in one of Gerard Manley Hopkins' poems. Hopkins was not exactly a feminist, so I wondered how this author was going to use that allusion in a story quite unlike any setting Hopkins ever used in his poetry. It took only the first page to get me involved.

On the first page, I learned that a main character was an artist and that she was on a journey. Within a few more pages, I realized that this story was something like *The Fires of Bride.* As Maria Milleny journeys from the city of London to the remote island of Cailleach to search out her mother's homeland, Carole (pronounced with three syllables), a main character in *Send My Roots Rain*, drives from the city of Brooklyn to the remote, anonymous border town of Pozo Seco, Texas, to learn more about the birth area of her father. Her father had been born and raised near Pozo Seco.

Then the story takes on its own form. When he was old enough, he left the area for Brooklyn, changed his name from *Rio* to *Riff* and refused to speak his mother tongue, Spanish, though he married a woman from Spain. Carole wants to know why he did all that.

She could not learn from him because he quit speaking to her when she told him she was lesbian; he even cut her out of his will. Her mother and seven siblings supported her, but they could not answer her question about why the father was so ashamed of his heritage. Being cut from his will does not trouble her; his being ashamed of his heritage does, and she wants to know why. Needing to know her father's heritage is the catalyst that prompts her to answer an ad in an art magazine placed by the priest in Pozo Seco who is looking for an artist to paint murals on his church walls. Answering the ad begins Carole's journey.

Carole is on the kind of journey that seems contradictory; it is a journey to find meaning in her life as a woman in the patriarchy as well as a journey to find her power as a woman through discovering the missing piece to her Self by searching for her *paternal* ancestral roots. It is a journey to discover how to do both in a culture that does not support the quest. What else is fascinating about the quest in this particular story is that, though Carole searches for paternal ancestry, the search takes her into an almost totally woman-centered community; the only male who surfaces as a character having more than a few lines is the town's priest, and his role is marginalized. Other men are referred to only in passing.

As I read even the first few pages of this story, I was reminded of a passage by Virginia Woolf when she mused:

> "Chloe liked Olivia," I read. And then it struck me how immense a change was there. Chloe liked Olivia perhaps for the first time in literature. Cleopatra did not like Octavia. And how completely *Antony and Cleopatra* would have been altered had she done so . . . how interesting it would have been if the relationship between the two women had been more complicated.[38]

Though Carole is on this quest for her paternal roots, immediately Gómez-Vega places her in a relationship that mirrors Chloe and Olivia by extending Woolf's idea so that "Chloe" not only liked "Olivia" but the core community that influences that relationship is woman-centered: Carole (as Chloe), Maria Soledad (as Olivia), Cora, Miriam, another Maria, and female children, Zemi, Clarita and Luz, as well as women who influence the others but who are not present in Pozo Seco—Carole's, Maria Soledad's and Cora's mothers. The English language has phrases for groups: a gaggle of geese, a pride of lions, a pod of whales. If there is a name for a group of women like this, it would be called a "weave."[39]

That word *weave*, as both noun and verb, precisely describes the interactions of the women in this story. Before beginning the actual process of weaving, a weaver needs to thread the loom through heddles. The action of threading is called "warping." The warp threads are the vertical ones, the horizontal ones, the woof. To weave, the weaver fills the shuttles— bobbin-like spools— with thread and passes the shuttles horizontally through the warp, using pedals or lifts to raise selected warped threads while others remain lowered. The process of raising and lowering the warp threads and passing the shuttles through forms the pattern.

This process describes the actions of the women in this story, for Gómez-Vega gives the many women characters in her novels the same kind of equal responsibility for the successes of each other's lives as the weaver does the threads of the weave. In fact, at times she makes each of them a first-person narrator—of their lives and sometimes the lives of those in the town.

All of the women narrators in the story hold strands of threads that weave in and out through each others' lives. They all share actively in the outcome of those lives. Although Carole's quest to find the part of her that is missing by finding out more about her father makes her *a* principal narrator, she is not *the* principal narrator; she does not dominate the pattern of the story. All the women in this story are simultaneously the weavers and the threads.

The male figure present in the story is the priest who will decide if Carole's work shows the artistry he wants for his church walls. Her paintings of famous people and famous buildings look stiff and boring.[40] What he likes the most are her paintings of lions, likes them enough to hire her. As the priest looks over the canvases covered with lions, she ponders her images:

> There were lions in motion, chasing their prey or being chased, and there were lions stretched the full length of their bodies in the shade of a tree. There were lions that seem to be smiling,

looking over a cliff, and there were lions waiting, maybe to be
slaughtered and hung on my father's wall. . . . I was drawing my
nightmares on the canvas. (18–19)

Her lion dream/nightmare is always the same: several lions
(sometimes one) would stalk her for a while, swishing their tails
close enough to hit her, roar in her face, then chase her to a cliff,
sending her over the edge to free fall. She would wake up before
hitting the ground "with the emptiness that dreaming of such
things always left in me." (91)

Her paintings of buildings and famous people occupy only the
profane space of her creativity. Painting the lions is the muted call
of Earth wanting to story her to wholeness.

Carole knows that she wants to exorcise the negative influence that her father has on her, the control he has over her when
she feels vulnerable and weak. She feels that if she knew of his heritage, she could gain her own control. Besides denying his heritage, the other thing that bothers Carole about her father is that
he used to hunt game in exotic places and send the stuffed heads of
the animals back home. He especially liked to kill lions.

As the story goes on, Maria Soledad's life and Cora's life come
to the fore and Carole's life fades into the background. Like Carole,
Maria and Cora are from Hispanic backgrounds; like Carole, they
are fluent in Spanish and English, Maria also in Portuguese and
French; they are close friends; unlike Carole, they have both
entered the United States illegally. Cora is a prostitute who cannot
read, though Maria nags at her to learn day after day. Maria has a
Bachelor's degree in philosophy from a university in Brazil, her
birthplace. Maria's confidante is Miriam, a *curandera* whom Father
Arroyo calls *bruja*, Spanish for witch, whom he forbids Maria to
see; as a Hispanic *curandera* in a border town, Miriam is loved by
the people in ways that Father Arroyo is not, and he uses his influence as priest to keep Miriam at arm's length from the townspeo-

ple. Since Father Arroyo is also Maria Soledad's employer and thus the one who keeps her from financial poverty (she is his housekeeper), Maria visits Miriam in secret. (222–27)

Thus the warp and woof are developing together. A mention that the old church has burned down and a new one has not yet been built makes the responsive reader and Carole, the outsider, wonder why she was hired to paint murals on church walls that do not exist. A mention of "Luz and her death in the fire" (22) makes the reader blink and ask, "What did I miss?" The reader missed nothing. Luz has been brought into the circle the way the others have been brought in: in the middle with no introduction.

After giving tantalizing pieces of information about Cora, Maria, and Miriam, Gómez-Vega drops those threads and brings Carole back into the story. Here is where we learn that Carole's mother is from Spain, having come to the United States during World War II, that her mother has died recently, and that her death plunged Carole and her seven siblings into darkness: "she had been our light, and not having her with us left us in darkness." (29). We learn that Cora and Carole live at the same inn in town, the only inn. (28–29) We also learn that there is another Maria who will be important as a narrator: two Marias.

All of this background explanation, the warp, is necessary in order to understand the conflicts and complexities of the stories of these women. In the art and craft of weaving, the weaving itself could be called the least important part of the entire process. Warping a loom sometimes can take not only hours but days. Deciding on the pattern in the background or warp threads and then threading the heddles determine the success of the product. Unlike other needlework projects, setting background takes precedence over everything else; sometimes it can be tedious and painfully slow, but if the product is to be beautiful, it is mandatory that the weaver show care, discernment, and precision.

I see Gómez-Vega taking the same kind of care to warp the background for her characters to emerge fully believable. Taking that care helps to make Gómez-Vega a reliable narrator for me so that as I read the story of this community of women I can find truth in their ways.

The warp threads continue to be chosen and loomed: the second Maria is added. (31) In fact, she is first added as a "her": "someone should write to her," (31) We learn that the second Maria and Miriam are good friends, that she is jealous of Maria Soledad and that Maria Soledad took the job as the priest's housekeeper to leave Miriam's house, where she was living, to quiet the jealousy.

In the early chapters of the story, we gain insight and information into the nature of the women's weave: Maria Soledad, Cora, Miriam, Maria Selena, even six-year-old Zemi. We wonder at these women and the way they work so closely in each others' lives: they give each other orders; they yell; they are opinionated; they fight; and they love each other very much. They begin to include Carole, the outsider, because she is the catalyst who starts the rebuilding of the church.

When the church burned down, the second Maria, Maria Selena, placed a curse on the town that could be lifted only by an outsider, or so these people think: they are people steeped in many old, old traditions, some traditions becoming superstitions.

The woman who cursed the town did so when her daughter Luz burned to death in the fire that destroyed the church. She returns to Pozo Seco after the church has been rebuilt at the request of Maria Soledad and Miriam. Five years have passed since the fire. Five years since the crowd held her back from entering the flaming building, not believing her that Luz was in the church. Five years since she broke with Miriam for not divulging the vision of Luz in flames. Five years since the people treated her and Luz as outcasts because Luz's father was the local priest whom Father Arroyo replaced after a scandal started from knowledge of the paternity. Five years since she cursed the people for allowing Luz to die in the fire.

The curse worked. No one would rebuild the church until an outsider came to begin the process of rebuilding. Maria Soledad writes to Maria Selena to tell her that the church is rebuilt with an outsider's help (Carole) and that the first mass will be offered for Luz. She asks Maria Selena to return to Pozo Seco and heal the wounds that have festered among everyone in the town for the years since she left. Only Maria Selena, by forgiving the townspeople, can heal those wounds. As she steps down from the train that brings her back to Pozo Seco after the five-year absence, she thinks about how those years had to pass "before . . . she could accept that Miriam had been as powerless as she was to prevent Luz's death." (94)

Miriam, the *curandera*, "was the voice of prophecy." (57) Not only does she help cure the sick, she has visions. Miriam saw Luz enveloped in flames even before she was born: "how could she tell Maria that her only child would suffer so?" (57) All Miriam would tell her friend before the birth was, "Name her Luz," (58) Spanish for *light*. The priest finds Miriam evil because he cannot control her: Maria Soledad tells him, "You're afraid of her, but she's not afraid of you." (112) She lives in a house in the desert, on the edge of town and does not go to church. To Maria and Zemi and Cora, she is like a mother—she was Maria's midwife at Zemi's birth—one who is trustworthy and consoling. To Maria Selena, she is the quintessence of love and friendship. To Carole, she appears to be a woman who has inner personal power whose influence extends through the town in a positive way to everyone but the priest.

Another important character in the story is Maria Soledad's closest friend, Cora, a prostitute who, at twenty-eight, is unable to read or write. She has crossed the Texas/Mexico border illegally with the help of what the border people call "the coyote." Many coyotes take women across the border at deserted spots for a fee, then rape these women and abandon them in the desert. Some die. Some do not. Some, like Cora, become pregnant from the rape.

Almost no woman fights and struggles with a coyote because they would be killed. Cora fights her coyote, however, fights him with his own knife, turning on him and slashing his belly.

Because she has crossed with only the clothes on her back and no money in her pockets, she becomes a prostitute as a way to survive. When her daughter, Clarita, is born, Cora sends her to live with her mother because Cora does not make enough money to support two people.

Cora's struggle within herself, however, is not because she is a prostitute; it is because she has a desire to be a painter, and to her understanding of the world, there will never be a way that she can act on that desire. Cora is a *mestiza*, which means that she was instilled with the notion that the ideal woman is one "who stands behind her man in silence and passivity. . . . To study, read, paint, write are not legitimate choices for the mestiza," even in the late twentieth-century.[41] At twenty-eight "she has nothing to show for her many bruises, and they were beginning to hurt." (43) At twenty-eight and now a Tejana (a *mestiza* or Chicana living in Texas) she feels the pull away from her *mestiza* role and toward her potential as a painter.

Like Carole, something in Cora's past that she cannot acknowledge blocks her from becoming a more self-confident woman who owns her personal power, who heeds her own voice. Her friend Maria offers many times to teach Cora to read; she will not accept the offer. Maria keeps suggesting that Cora send for her daughter; so does Miriam; but she will not. Cora tells Maria that she no longer even dreams, a story that Maria will not accept.

The word "dream" is used in two different ways in this story: one describes the images, the plans that some of the women have for the future. These dreams are future-oriented, pointing to a better life for the dreamer. "Better" can mean wanting a higher income, a bigger house, a promotion, advanced degrees. The other way that "dream" is used is connected with "visions," such as the ones that Carole has when she images her lions, or the dream/visions that Miriam has when she can see the future. The first type of dream points to a *better* life; the second to a *way* of life, a path to follow. Cora is referring to the first definition of dreams.

Cora's sending for her daughter would not be a simple act, of course, because her dilemma is not only that she has almost no confidence in her innate drives and abilities, but that she has a mother similar to Gertie's in *The Dollmaker*: a mother who is "a cruel, callous woman." (44) In the weave, the mother is a thread that entangles rather than weaves itself with the threads of her daughter, Cora, and Cora's daughter, Clarita. That entanglement, for part of the story, pulls the rest of the weave off-balance until the thread of Cora's mother is broken so that it is no longer woven through the lives, the stories, of Cora and Clarita, or of Cora's friends who have seen the harm from the entanglement.

Cora's mother, born about 1940 in an isolated desert town in Mexico, was trained to accept what she was told to do: to be obedient, not to argue. She was trained not to want to be anything but a housewife, to do anything but to serve her husband and her church.[42] She was pressed into service as a prostitute at an early age, and if, indeed, any creativity longed to express itself, there was no time for that expression. She, in turn, pressed her daughter Cora into service at an early age, forcing her onto the streets at the age of fourteen to earn money for the household.

We are not told what finally moves Cora to go against her mother and send for her daughter. Reading between the lines, I surmise that the pivotal moment is when Maria tells Cora that Cora's mother would do to Clarita what she did to Cora: Cora's mother never sent Cora to school, and, when Cora was just old enough, she "threw her out in the streets." (44) Thus, Cora was an experienced prostitute when she crossed the border. Yet this was the same environment in which Cora placed her daughter. Why? With so little self-confidence that she could not find enough money to rear her daughter, she left her daughter with the person who had stolen her power before she knew she had any: her mother. When

Maria reminds her that the life Cora has run away from is the same one that Cora placed her daughter in, Cora begins to have a vision of her daughter grown: illiterate and a prostitute.

Carol Christ believes that, "Women need stories that will tell them that their ability to face the darkness in their lives is an indication of strength, not weakness."[43] Cora needs stories, needs them more than food, and she needs a friend like Maria to tell them to her. The stories and the friend push Cora to call for her daughter. In so doing, Cora begins to take back her own power; she begins to be whole; she begins to heal. Her new sense of Self roots her in a new reality; that new reality says, "I have powers as a woman in this universe of which I am an important part." Cora's confidence level soars to a point that allows her to play a major role in completing the murals on the church walls.

Maria knows that, in the privacy of her rented room, Cora sketches and draws. She knows that Cora needs to earn money other than through prostitution if she is to reunite with her daughter. So it is Maria who suggests to Cora that she ask Carole if she could be her assistant. The call is voiced.

Asking Carole to be her assistant is as difficult for Cora to act on as is sending for her daughter. She explains to Carole why it is difficult: "You think wishes come true." "'Mine never have,' said Carole. 'Yours?'" Cora answers, "'Not unless I've shed something for them. You know, like a lizard.' . . . I think I'm shedding my skin right about now.'" (129) Before the reader's eyes, Cora is renewing her spirit, for in the symbolism of the goddess story, reptiles shedding skin is a sign of life's renewal, of reincarnation; the shedding of the skin implies rebirth.[44]

Cora starts her apprenticeship slowly, observing, hesitating to mix colors, to apply paint to brush. In the end, she is the one who finishes painting the murals because Carole is in the desert fighting her lions, and the priest has scheduled a mass for Luz: she is on a deadline. The entire community of Pozo Seco is awed by Cora's ability to finish the project in the absence of her mentor. "'You should be proud,' Maria tells her. Cora obviously was. She had worked on these walls for months, and in the process she had become an artist, a woman sure of herself and what she wanted." (188) Cora sheds her skin and is reborn, because she realizes that she has a Self that identifies her as more than an illiterate prostitute.

One of the human, innate drives that Tillie Olsen lists is the drive to create. Cora's drive is to create paintings, not misery. When she answers the call of that drive, her process of rebirth begins. When she begins to paint, she abandons prostitution because Carole pays her part of her own salary, enough to support Cora and her daughter. She also learns to read. Like the mythic Demeter in search of Persephone, Cora pushes herself past the point in her life where she feels powerless and actively seeks to bring her daughter back to her. When Clarita returns to her mother, Cora discovers that Maria's insights are correct; Cora's mother did not use the money Cora sent her for Clarita to learn to read and write and have decent clothes. When Clarita returns to her mother at the age of six, she can neither read nor write, and she is shabbily dressed.

Like Maria Milleny, Cora has made a journey into herself to find out and face what it is that does not allow her to grow. She is not physically dying, but she has ceased to be alive, and most important, open to change. Cora's metaphor of shedding her skin is an appropriate metaphor for her, because her tough exterior that has gotten her through life thus far, is the same tough exterior that impeded her growth. She cannot break through her own toughness until she has a dream/vision of her daughter grown.

The other woman who is stagnating in her spiritual life is Maria Soledad. As Father Arroyo's housekeeper, she cooks his meals, cleans the house, and is paid a meager salary, augmented by free room and board for her and Zemi. During her pregnancy and the birth, she lived with Miriam, because Miriam found her coming from the desert, took her in and cared for her. Like Cora, Maria crossed the border illegally. Unlike Cora, she was not raped by a coyote. Zemi is a love child.

Maria is a wonderful facilitator for her friends: she knows when and how to push Cora into change; she brings Luz's mother, Maria Selina, back to the town she has fled from five years ago after the fire; she is an excellent housekeeper for Father Arroyo, never delaying supper, always cleaning. But she has done nothing to nourish and feed her Self's growth since she came to Pozo Seco about seven years ago.

Maria is the kind of woman whose stagnancy is difficult to see, because she seems to be busy, seems to be working and progressing. But like Carole and Cora, Maria has something in her past that she cannot face: the violent death of her mother and her mother's best friend. After the deaths of these two women, Maria had to flee her homeland even before the funerals; her life was not safe.

Maria's mother, Lola, a socialist in the '70s and '80s and her friend, Rebecca, a radical from London, were union organizers in Brazil. Maria's mother had been politically active for a long time, and she was well respected among the people she was organizing; they sought her out even on the beach or on the street: "They knew she wouldn't desert them," Maria tells Carole. (146) Maria's mother and Rebecca were gunned down in a brothel, trying to organize the prostitutes.

Unlike Cora and Carole, Maria knows what blocks the flow of her path to healing: she is unable to grieve. She tells Carole, "I want them to be alive, for themselves and for Zemi. . . . I try not to think about them because it doesn't make any sense that they should be dead, and because I can't handle it." (152) Maria is running from her past: she cannot confront it, learn how it is taking her power, how it is keeping her from developing the spirit side of herself. Her spirit died with her mother's body.

Death of the old self must take place before rebirth of a new Self is possible; this is a truth known and tested for millennia. We know of life, death, and rebirth from the cycles of the moon, the cycles of the seasons, the growth and loss of the leaves on the trees, the shedding of skins, the changing of temperatures. Before any human recorded the changes and cycles, they were already taking place. Indigenous tribes live by a cyclic spirituality that accept death as part of the life cycle and accept that the death of a body does not erase the life of the spirit that inhabited that body. Alice Walker writes of this truth:

> If there is one thing African-Americans and Native Americans have retained of their African and ancient American heritages, it is . . . the belief that everything is inhabited by spirit. This belief encourages knowledge perceived intuitively.[45]

Paula Gunn Allen says that at one time for Native Americans, the primary value was relationship to the spirit world: "it was at one time the primary value of all tribal people on earth."[46] Being Brazilian, Maria acknowledges the strong presence of the spirit world within the physical world. She understands that, though her mother's body is dead, her spirit is not. But she does not *acknowledge* this wisdom, and almost ten years later, she has not completed the grieving over the death of her mother's physical body; however, before leaving the country, she had seen her mother's body and had counted the thirty-eight holes from the thirty-eight bullets that had pierced it. (145)

As answering the ad in the paper became a catalyst for Carole to change, Carole's presence and subsequent friendship and love became a catalyst for Maria to change. Their friendship stirs up visions for Maria of the friendship that Maria's mother and Rebecca experienced. The visions, not as sight images but as feelings, cause Maria to change, to have doubts about her present condition. Not since she arrived in Pozo Seco almost a decade before, had Maria told her complete story to anyone, not even Miriam.

It is the *telling* of her story to Carole that helps Maria unblock her stagnation. Leaving Brazil did not uproot her; being unable to grieve did. "Grief dares us to love once more,"[47] but Maria is neither ready to grieve nor ready to love. Though it is Carole who cries out in the night, "Mine, O Thou lord of life, send my roots rain," (91) Maria's roots need rain, too. Her mother and her mother's activities and personality gave Maria her groundedness as Carole's mother has given Carole her light. With the retrospective, with the telling of her story to Carole, Maria realizes that she has not formed an identity separate from that of "her mother's daughter," and she needs to form that identity before she can develop a bond with Carole. "But, reflected Carole, she [Maria] didn't have half her [mother's] courage." (192) Carole was willing to weave the strand of her life in and through Maria's, but Maria could not reciprocate.

Unblocking a path, facing a past that is troubled or violent, does not come easily. There are setbacks as the person longs for comfort in the familiar. Maria is no different. She plans to return to Brazil with Zemi, not to "go home again," but as a way to avoid the present. Maria wants life boundaried by the familiar details of the physical world of childhood. Then she will not need to push through the other area in her life that fills her with discomfort: her growing relationship with Carole.

Not only does Chloe like Olivia, Olivia likes Chloe. As the story unfolds, Maria finally admits to the depth of Carole's and her love as she begins to feel strong in herself. She still fears the unknown, but her life now will be supported by Carole, Zemi, Cora and Clarita, for all of them will form a new community within the larger community of Pozo Seco: they are moving into their own house, and they will support each other. Maria Soledad is no longer financially so dependent on the priest that her employment there precludes her healing. The memories, the experiences and the town's milieu form a new warp; the strands of the five females, and the strands of Miriam, Maria Selena, and Father Arroyo, will form a new woof of the weave.

Maria's struggle is an understandable one. Many of her life experiences parallel her mother's experience. As Zemi is a love child born to Maria and a fellow college student who crossed the desert with her, so was Maria the love child of her mother and father, born when both of them were in college. Maria's mother came to love a woman, Rebecca, when Rebecca came from England to Brazil. So too Maria. Then would Maria meet death as her mother did? That question, irrational though it may seem to outsiders, preys upon Maria's mind. Pozo Seco, Texas, however, is not a place for the kind of violence that killed Maria's mother.

In addition, Maria might have seemed to be just like her mother, but she is not. Lola was a political activist while a student at the university; Maria is neither an activist nor a union organizer. She is, however, a personal organizer, the facilitator who moves other women to personal, life-changing action.

As weaver-narrator, she moves her strand and those of the others through a background of Catholic fundamentalism, native superstition, and homophobia. Was her mother killed because she was politically active, an unmarried mother, or openly loving another woman? "Maria remembered that the newspaper had called her mother a whore even in death." (145) Maria's personal truth becomes both political and public when the colors of the background make their impression on the foreground. The color of her thread in the past was muted and soft. Admitting to her past and her grief, and in so doing finding her own Self as standing out of the shadow of her mother, changes the color of her thread in the cloth to a vibrant and bright one, while still entwined with the warp.

As the outsider who enters the circle of life in Pozo Seco, Carole is the catalyst who moves the people to rebuild the church, who moves Cora to consent to have Maria teach her to read, to assist in painting the walls, and to send for her daughter. She is the catalyst who brings Maria Selene back to Pozo Seco to shed her grief and renew her friendship with Maria Soledad and Miriam. She is even the catalyst who softens the heart of Father Arroyo to accept Miriam. And it is the ad in the newspaper in Brooklyn for someone to paint murals on a wall of a church in the birth area of her father that was the catalyst for Carole's change.

Knowing all that helped me to understand what Carol Christ discovered about women, power and spirituality in writing of the main female character in Margaret Atwood's *Surfacing*:

> The heroine's understanding that her power stemmed from her clear understanding of *her rooting in nature and in her own personal past* [emphasis mine] provided me with an alternative notion of power as insight and grounding . . . that achievement of authentic selfhood and power depends on understanding one's grounding in nature and natural energies.[48]

Carole has several catalysts working to give *her* a "clear understanding of her rooting in nature." Through conversations between Carole and Maria, the reader learns of Maria's past and Carole's past. It is in one of those conversations that we learn of Carole's need to find "her own personal past": as Carole explains her relationship with her father, she thinks to herself, "I wasn't sure that . . . Maria would know what it meant to have no ancestry." (68) Carole knows her maternal ancestry, but it is not enough. Where are her paternal roots?

Though she labors alongside the men who build the new church and feels close to them, she does not feel connected to the town or her work: "Carole contemplated the green cacti . . . the . . . greenery in this desert land . . . and they reminded her that everything and everyone around her were somehow thriving, flourishing. Unlike her." (71) Carole perceives herself as sterile, and that which is sterile cannot create.

Pozo Seco enters the rainy season as the laborers finish the church. Rain is Carole's new excuse for not beginning the walls: "I had been in Pozo Seco for several months . . . and I hadn't yet determined what my purpose was. Painting the walls was just a job. . . . It didn't seem right that drops of rain should have a purpose when I didn't." (76) The purpose of rain is to fall, thought Carole, and in falling and penetrating the earth, nourish and feed the roots of plants, trees—and people.

One of the bar patrons at the inn gives her insight into another purpose for rain. He joins Carole at her table one evening when she is eating supper. "'It's raining,' said Carole. 'Yeah. . . . And a good thing, too. The birds will be mating after this. . . . The whole damned desert'll be fucking. . . . Yeah, . . . they needs the rain for that. . . . They don't do nothing if it don't rain.'" (77) "'What if it doesn't rain for a year?' Carole asked . . . "'They wait.' said Cora, having joined the conversation. . . . 'Why. . .?' 'So they can feed their young.'" (77–78) The rain draws out the birds, invisible and silent during the long, hot, dry season. (78) This interchange and the insight brings not joy but sadness to Carole, because now she realizes that, indeed, "when the rain stops, . . . the desert'll bloom." (79) But not Carole, because she perceives that the kind of rain she needs to be nourished does not fall from the sky.

With these feelings of sadness over her lack of purpose in life, the lions return both in her imagination and in her dreams: "When I opened the door to my room, there was a lion on my bed." (81)

We learn in the opening chapter that Carole does her best art work when she draws lions. (18) We also learn that she draws her nightmares on canvas when she draws lions. (19) However, the priest didn't want lions on the walls; he wants religious scenes.

I was now realizing that Carole was searching for something other than finding an answer to the nagging question about where her father is from. She needed to know, "who am I, and how am I connected to the cosmos?" The very questions I was asking.

No wonder she cannot paint. In her dreams reside the darkness and chaos that hold terror for her. However, she does not yet know that the darkness and chaos need not be feared, that they are other sides of the Self, and that uncovering the Self can be empowering; it need not be met with fear. But for the time being, "in the state I was in, . . . I didn't have the energy to deal with my demons, then." (81–82) Nor did she have the desire. However, she has walls to paint, walls that will hold religious murals to fulfill the contract she signed with the priest, and, indirectly, the town.

It is Maria who helps Carole begin that task as she talks with her about painting into the murals the faces of the people of Pozo Seco: the people who had helped to build the church and the ones who came to watch the church being built. It is Maria who fills in the spaces behind the faces of the people: "The stories Maria told me were the difference between the drawings on these walls and the stuff I'd done before I came to Pozo Seco. If nothing else, she gave my work depth." (108) This "depth" is the kind that comes only from knowing the stories and thus understanding the reasons for the laugh lines near the corners of the eyes; the worry lines etched between the eyebrows above the bridge of the nose; the bend in the shoulders that speaks of the weight of years or too many burdens in life: "fire in those faces . . . that passion could ignite . . . a look of commitment." (108) Carole had decided to also have Christ resemble the townspeople: he is brown, "like themselves, . . . His cross had become their own. His resurrection likewise theirs." (108)

Carole's path to find her personal ancestry is made clearer, again by Maria, on a picnic in a national park in the Guadalupe Mountains. Maria begins to question Carole about Carole's fear and distrust of the desert:

> "He used to send us stupid cards of the desert. . . . The man was out killing these animals and he sent pictures. He also shipped home the heads of the animals he shot during his little trips. . . . I sort of carry it [the desert on the cards] with me everywhere I go." Replies Maria, "Because it's your past, your history." (151)

In searching for her father's heritage in the region where he was born, Carole opens herself to confront an unknown history that could contain tragedy. Otherwise, why would her father tear up his bioregional roots and, for all practical purposes, allow them to wither and die? But confront she must if she is to regain her personal power that, through no fault of her own, was stolen from her before she was born. Carol Christ's definition of power as insight and grounding kept returning to me as I realized that Carole wants to reclaim that stolen power, lost through her father's willful uprooting and silence.

Maria points out that Carole's lions are about her father and his lack of acceptance of her: "He's the one who shot them and hung them on his walls. . . . Maybe you feel he shot you down, too." (159) Thus Carole begins to understand that her nightmares of lions and her feelings for her father are linked.

The next evening, Carole decides to face her lions and finds only one: "'He fixed me with his eyes and rose to shake his head. The hair on his mane, much like my own, stood on end, then fell about the sides . . . his agile body taut like my own runner's legs. 'You look so much like me,' I told him. And he pounced.'" (163) Now the lion resembles Carole as Maria Melleny's seaweed-woman resembled her. But, from Carole's perspective, her lion is a terrible and fierce animal that can harm her.

To help her character through the darkness that obscures her vision's path, Gómez-Vega creates a conflict: Maria cannot find Zemi and she fears that she has gone into the desert, forbidden territory to the child. Knowing Carole's fears about the desert, Maria asks Carole to return to the house in the event that Zemi shows up there. For Carole, darkness does not mean the absence of light; darkness has become equated with the desert. She is terrified of the desert; she finds it too huge, too frightening, too dangerous. She has publicly announced to everyone since she came to Pozo Seco that she fears the desert: "I was hoping and praying that she wouldn't ask me to go with her. . . . Nothing, not even Maria could get me to enter that desert." (171–72) She cannot yet make the connection between desert and nightmares even though the lion heads her father sent home belong to lions that were all killed in deserts.

Zemi shows up at her home where Carole is waiting for her. After putting her to bed and placing Father Arroyo in charge, Carole decides to search for Maria and tell her that Zemi is safe: "A journey into the desert was not something I would be good at, but the thought of Maria in danger made me decide to risk it all." (175)

That decision to risk it all is shored up by a stop at the church. As Carole passes the church on the way to the desert, "the light of the moon seemed to be illuminating the altar from inside." (176) By the way the windows were built, that kind of illumination is in fact impossible. The light makes Carole wonder if Luz has returned. After the fire, Luz's mother prophesied that Luz would return one day, and Miriam asks Father Arroyo, in an unfriendly debate in the church when she has come to visit Carole, "You think I can find the devil here. Why not something else? Why not Luz?"(110)

Carole enters the church, drawn in by more than the illumination. Perhaps, she thinks, Cora is showing the church "at this hour." (176) Since Carole took Cora on as an assistant, Cora has not only "given up her previous trade, . . . she had also started dropping by the church on Sundays with Clarita . . . [to show] her creation to the women." (176) As this woman passes from one window to the other, "she took the images along. . . . I became almost certain, for the first time, that it must be Luz." (176)

Carole calls to Luz, to tell her that she has made the murals for her. "I painted all the faces of the people you knew, so you wouldn't be alone. Carole's last sentence to Luz is, "Help me find her": (177) "her" meaning Maria.

Carole thinks she hears Maria's voice calling to her, so she runs out of the church to follow the call of the voice and comes "face to face with the desert." (177) Scared, confused, she then calls on the only other person she trusts: her mother. "'Mother,' I called. 'Guide me.' I had no concept of a religious world, but I knew that my mother, as one of the ancestors who looked after my soul, could be depended upon to guide me." (177)

Guides are necessary when we make our journey into our Selves. On the one hand, we make the journey alone, because only we can know the moment when we root to our inner core and become whole again; on the other hand, communality and support in the journeying are part of every indigenous tradition. The support comes via our spirit and our animal guides. Thus, following a primal tradition, Carole reaches into that tradition to call upon two spirit guides, two females: her mother and Luz.

Ready to sacrifice her need for safety and her fear of the desert/darkness, Carole goes to search for Maria: "I knew that my mother would understand, so I closed my eyes and took the first few steps. . . . When I opened my eyes, I was in the desert." (177)

Carole walks through the night calling Maria's name. When her calls are answered "only by the flurry of fluttering wings," she thinks they are bats. (178) Flickering fingers of light spreading out of the sun "become steel rakes that cut up the ground." (178) When she sees a man in the distance on top of the mountain, she does not think that someone was rescuing her; she thinks, "'A coyote!' . . . Cora's story of her rape came back to me all too clearly." (179) The ground moves in front of her, it seems: "my tired body bolted and ran . . . something was after me." (179)

What is so fearsome to Carole in the region is what she fears most in herself: the vast emptiness and eternal silence of the desert. The fear of the external emptiness of the desert mirrors the fear of the emptiness in her creativity.

Into the second day, and without food and water, Carole begins to make bargains: "if only Maria—or anyone—would find me, . . . I would put this insane escapade out of my mind . . . get in my car and take off . . . down a *previously charted path*." [emphasis mine] (179) Fear of the unknown is one of the ways that the lions have gotten to Carole. That falls into place with her overriding fear:

fear of what she will find if and when she faces the terror that is her Self, the Self of the desert, the shadows, the place of eternal silence.

Just as she makes the bargain for rescue and a previously charted path, from out of nowhere, a lion springs: "I fell backwards on the ground . . . its body, sometimes bigger than life, reducing me to nothingness. . . . I could feel . . . the heat of his body merging with mine, but I didn't care. I was hoping for the end." (180) The end does not come. When Carole awakens the next morning, she is still among the living. However, since she has had neither food nor water for two days and nights, she is weak and her skin begins to peel: "I'm becoming a pillar of sand. . . . And what for. . . . I hadn't even dared look back when I wasn't supposed to. . . . Women looked back, like Lot's wife, and what was usually left of us was nothing but a sand pile." (184)

Lot's wife carries special meaning to both Carole and Maria. Carole has read a revisionist poem to Maria about why Lot's wife looked back: "Because of her neighbors, her animals. She couldn't just leave them to their death. She had to look back. . . . Lot's wife had chosen death over a lonely exile. . . . Anything was preferable, she said." (184)

This poem describes Carole as well as Lot's wife. In *Carole's* interpretation, from *her* point of view, not going into the desert for Maria is the equivalent of not looking back. And death is better than lonely exile. Carole and Maria decide that at one point in both their lives, they left and did not look back, "because one did as one was told," and for both of them, it made them feel "disconnected from home." (184) Part of Carole's growth into wholeness, then, comes when she defies those who told her what is "right" for her and decides what is right for herself. That decision leads her to confront the terror of her emptiness, symbolized by the desert.

When she finally finds some water, and when a lion tries to trip her and obstruct her path to the water, Carole "simply walked through him when I had to." (185) She and this lion spend the rest of the day and night near the pool. What is different about this third night in the desert is that even though the man on top of the mountain "had a perfect view of me," she "finally lay down, this time of my own free will, and went to sleep." (185) The other two nights, she slept only because exhaustion forced her into sleep, not because she chose to sleep. Carole begins to name and claim what is important to her—in this instance, water and a space to rest without worry. Even her perception that she is in physical danger becomes less important than her need to claim space in which to be nourished and rested.

Simultaneously with Carole in the desert fighting her lions, the story line of Maria's experience continues. In a weave, Carole and her lion would be on one side; Maria, Cora, Zemi, Father Arroyo, Miriam and Maria Selene on the other. The middle would be warp on background, with shades of the countless and brilliantly-colored flowers blooming in the desert after the rains.

Maria returns to the house and learns from Cora that Carole is absent. The murals need to be finished for the upcoming mass for Luz. Cora needs Carole: "She calls all the shots." (181) The town is centering all of its energy on the mass. The mass will be a cleansing ritual, cleansing the townspeople of the guilt they have borne these five years since Luz's death. It will be an evening mass so that candles and the moon can light the way.

Cora finishes the walls without Carole, and in so doing, learns to make her own decisions. In the past, someone has prodded her to do this or that. Her life was not her own. Now, after working on the walls for months, having to make all of the final decisions, Cora admits to Maria, "I love these walls. . . . I have so much to thank them for." (188) The walls are living because they, too, have spirits in them.

Just before the time of the procession we learn that Carole is going to be all right: "She's being watched over," Miriam tells Maria Soledad. (188) The man on the mountain top is not a coyote but a friend of Miriam's; they are from the same Indian tribe. However,

Carole does not know that she will be all right, so her struggle is still a struggle in the emptiness.

What Carole misses by being in the desert is the finishing of the walls, Luz's mass, and the dying of an outmoded order of life so that an order that meets the needs of those involved may come forth: in an action that is not precluded by explanation, Father Arroyo kisses the hands of Miriam and Maria Selene as the mass begins, healing the wound that he created in himself by not accepting Miriam in his life and the church's life. That act also acknowledges to Miriam that, as a religious symbol of the Catholic patriarchy, he is ready to agree that Miriam's role in the town is as important as his; for Father Arroyo, a paradigmatic shift in thinking has occurred.

However, Carole is not quite ready to complete the healing process. Besides, her presence is not needed at the mass. She has been a catalyst, and as catalyst she accelerated changes. As catalyst, responsibility is not to be there when the reaction is accomplished. Her responsibility is now to herself.

Back in the desert, another lion roars into sight, followed by "desert warriors, their weapons drawn and anger on their faces—the grimaced faces of lion-haunted men." (189) Weaker, more vulnerable, Carole feels that she is losing the battle as the lion again pounces and knocks her over. If death was close the first night, it is even closer this fourth night. The lion roars so close to her face that she knows he is ready to swallow her, but he does not. Not swallowing her gives her a momentary impetus. She rises up from the ground, and the two of them circle each other. He knocks her down; she rises; he knocks her down; she rises, again and again. Up and down they go, "almost dancing, following his rhythm." (191) However, in what is to be the last attack, Carole accidentally falls on top of the lion instead of on the ground, "a shock to both of us, and I felt his body tense beneath mine, so I grabbed that sand-brown mane of his. 'Let me be!' I pleaded. He failed to roar this time, although I expected him to." (191)

When I was pondering this part of the story, I turned to my friend Joan Spencer to explain more fully what Carole was going through. Joan, from Mohawk and Lakota ancestry, is a pipe carrier and practices some of her traditions. She explained to me that in her traditions, an animal that appears in dreams as one who controls, like Carole's lions, is a representation of a person who is controlling the dreamer. This animal is called a power animal. The animal controls in the name of the person.

For Carole, the lion represents both her father and a side of her Self that she is afraid to acknowledge. In order for Carole to regain her power taken by the lions, she needs something from them. The controlling animal must give up something. Only then will the controlled person be able to regain the personal power lost, and then a relationship or connectedness of mutual being can begin.

Carole has pleaded with her lions many times before, and they have not given her back her power. However, she has never been in a conquering position with them; they were always been the ones "on top," knocking her to her knees, knocking her on her face, tripping her up so she would fall on her back and almost pass out.

With the pull of the mane, this lion surrenders, "as if he had been made of air. I rolled over on my back to release him. I wanted to conquer him, not kill him," (191) and he walks away into the light. The lion, then, does not give, say, a claw, a tooth, or a hank of hair. Rather, it is the act of Carole falling on top of him, of getting the better of him and physically pulling his hair that transfers power from him to her: "my eyes ached . . . and I cried silently for all the other lions who had, like him, been conquered only to hang, stuffed, on walls." (191)

Her *full* power has not returned yet, however. She has one more experience to finish the return: "the will of a force greater than my own . . . was moving . . . my body . . . falling off that cliff from which the lions had chased me countless times before throughout my life. . . . Laden with the weight of years, . . . my body hit the ground once and for all. . . . Crashing down felt like the wrath of years had conspired to grant me, at long last, peace." (191) Carole is healed. She is whole. Her personal power is fully hers for the first time in her life. She has met her demon and he returned to her what is rightfully hers: her Self. Carole had "a demon dance to perform," according to Miriam, (193) and she performed it bravely.

Carole is brought in to Father Arroyo's house by the same Indian who has been watching out for her while she danced in the desert. What Carole realizes about her lions and articulates to Maria is that "their comings and goings had a lot to do with how secure I felt about myself." (194) But she needed the vastness and emptiness of the desert, alone with her spirit guides, away from anything that could prop her up and help her to deny what is truly important for her, to realize what *is* important. Even the move from Brooklyn to Pozo Seco was not enough of a clearing out of props; she had to go to the desert to find what Carol Christ defined as "a clear understanding of her rooting in nature."

Her security as an artist comes to her with the painting of the church walls. Her security about herself comes with her winning the demon dance in the desert. She is a woman who has found power through "insight and grounding," a woman rooting self to Self, and as a reader, I walked her journey with her.

When Carole comes in from the desert, the threads that formed her life on one side of the warp and the threads that formed the lives on Zemi's, Maria's, Cora's, Clarita's, Miriam's and Maria Selene's side gradually merge to cover the warp; the women shuttle their threads back and forth to form a fabric that is strong and sup-porting. Not only does one contemporary woman root her Self in a particular culture, several of them do. The dream of Virginia Woolf, when she envisioned what would happen when a woman writer fleshed out the relationship between Chloe and Olivia, comes to life in the pages of this story where these women answer the call of their voices by mutually supporting and loving each other in a community that they decide to form by choice. Each will be entwined with the others, for richer or poorer, in sickness and in health. There are no gaps found in this weave.

Part II

Sacred Spaces:
the need to name and claim them in our lives

In her book *Sacred Dimensions of Women's Experience*, Elizabeth Dodson Gray writes that "naming the sacred" is essential to women because naming fosters the "power to shape reality into a form that serves the interests and goals of the one doing the naming."[1] Gray sees that naming-the-sacred is an activity that has been used as a way to separate men's work from women's work in heaven-centered religions with the idea that only men's work is sacred. Indeed, until recently, men have named the sacred in recorded Western history; Adam is the most famous namer, given the task to name the first animals.

Gray believes that "male naming in patriarchal religion has given us a strange landscape of the sacred. A *few* places, a *few* people, a *few* occasions are seen to concentrate and to embody the holy, and these stand like sacred mountains, inhabited by the elusive power of the world beyond." All else is "*un* holy" where ordinary people live their everyday lives. She goes on to state that this dualistic division was created for the purpose of getting away "from the ordinary, the natural, the unsacred—away from women, fleshy bodies, decaying nature, away from all that is rooted in mortality and dying."[2]

The sacred, as used by the male in patriarchal religious systems (and she includes here the authoritative religious texts of the Torah and the Koran as well as the Bible), was to lift the *men* out of the natural world and into a realm of transcendence, a realm "carved out, literally, over the bodies of women,"[3] "where nothing gets soiled, or rots, or dies."[4] That would exclude the" realms" of women's menstrual cycles, of mothering, of housekeeping, of gardening, and of growing old. Gray calls those few, specially chosen places that have been named as sacred by males, places that "shine with some of the magic of that sparkling transcendent stuff." She also "names" this process, "the old spiritual game . . . that the movement of holiness is up, the direction is away, and the motivation is to escape from 'here' to 'there.'"[5]

When women name the sacred, we go in the opposite directions from men, says Gray: instead of distancing ourselves and withdrawing from the reality of life to find sacredness, we go toward that reality—"toward bodies, toward nature, toward food, toward dust, toward transitory moments in relationships. And wherever we look, we find that which nourishes and deepens us."[6] Roots us. *Sacred*, then, is that which affirms life and my connections with something greater than I am. Women's naming of what is sacred "finds meaning in things that have never been found important."[7]

Reading Gray's insistence on naming the sacred, coupled with my desire to come to terms with how *sacred* fits into my search to find answers to the questions I was asking, I decided to research the etymological roots of *sacred*. I learned that *sacred* comes from *sacren*, to make holy, to consecrate, and from *sacer*, hallowed or to make holy. *Holy* comes from *hal* and is defined as "to make whole or to heal"; *whole, heal,* and *holy* come from the same root: *hal.* So, *sacred* is to make holy, and *holy* is that which is sacred or whole, to heal. Next I looked up *profane* and I found it defined as "a place or an object that is not holy."

Through this exercise, I was coming to realize that to name that-which-is-sacred is part of the construct of building a value system, and language is part of that value system. Words are not neutral. Thus the one-who-named-the-animals also created a value system, and he excluded what was sacred to women as well as excluding women-as-sacred.

Alice Walker calls this process of naming what is sacred, going "in search of our mothers' gardens" as she writes of the impact her mother and her foremothers have had on her philosophy and her writing:

> And perhaps in Africa, over two hundred years ago there was just such a mother; perhaps she painted vivid and daring decorations in oranges and yellows and greens on the walls of her hut; perhaps she sang—in a voice like Roberta Flack's—sweetly over the compounds of her village; perhaps she wove the most stunning mats or told most ingenious stories of all the village storytellers.[8]

These were the mothers who guided Alice's heritage "of a love of beauty and a respect for strength." That heritage Walker names as "sacred."

Space. What is "space"? Space, Gray says, is physical, as with gardens, rooms in the home, studios in cottages. Or it is relational, "found in families, in friendship, in support groups, in peace-making."[9] And both types are sacred.

Another "sacred space" that Gray describes and names is women's bodies: "Our women's bodies are the 'given' which we all share." In the process of sharing that given, "we also share a common vulnerability when we confront sexist advertising, pornography, rape, incest, battering, or about whether or not to abort." Whether our skin color is black, white, red, brown, or yellow, she feels that all women share the sacred spaces that are our bodies, and we are bound together in having had our female bodies declared unholy, profane, unclean by the patriarchal culture that has named the sacred for some thousand years. Thus Gray argues that women still "struggle to find sacred meaning where our culture [sees] no meaning."[10]

Another writer who affirms the need for "sacred" and "sacred space" is Luisah Teish, a priestess of the Yoruba tradition. In *Jambalaya: The Natural Woman's Book of Personal Charms and Practical Rituals*, she defines "sacred space" as "a place between the physical and spiritual world where the Ancestors and the living can communicate in peace."[11] In that space the rituals are performed that allow for the contact with the Ancestors. The Ancestors hold the power to change the reality of the person calling on them. The person calling lives in the physical, material world, the Ancestors in the spiritual world, and these Ancestors are alive. Toni Morrison agrees with Luisah Teish in believing that the Ancestors themselves are sacred: "when you kill the ancestors, you kill yourself."[12]

In Susan Jeffers' adaptation of the speech attributed to Chief Seattle, she quotes: "Every part of this earth is sacred to our people. Every pine needle. Every sandy shore. Every mist in the dark woods. . . . All are holy in the [ancestral] memory of our people." (np) Taking the adjectives of "sacred" and "holy" to be that which carries healing wholeness, then every creature and every part of Earth is "consecrated" and thus is to be treated with respect and esteem.

Paula Gunn Allen writes that "the word *sacred* . . . has a very different meaning to tribal people than to members of technological societies. It does not signify something of religious significance . . . but something that is filled with an intangible but very real power or force." She goes on to say that "ceremonial literature is sacred; it has power."[13] Thus "sacred" and "religious" have no ties to each other for Allen, as they do not have for Walker.

For Jeannette Armstrong, Okanagan, "our [tribe's] language comes from a sacred place . . . the vast pool of creation and origin. . . . When we consider the spiritual place from which our thinking arises, the words become sacred things because they come from that place."[14] As a writer, Armstrong feels a great responsibility to choose words that, instead of destroying, heal. Words have the power to destroy and the power to heal. (*Power* comes from *potere*: to be able.) Words, then, are sacred and powerful, filled with Allen's "intangible force."

The first-person narrator in *Surfacing* was looking for sacred spaces. She reflected that sacred spaces are "the places where you could learn the truth,"[15] thus following the path Eliade set down when he wrote: "the experience of sacred space makes a meaningful life possible."[16]

From my readings and conversions and reflections, then, I believe that naming spaces as sacred is necessary for a woman to define herself, understand herself, and know herself because that defining, understanding, and knowing informs her whole (healed) life. The space/place in which she finds wholeness/healing is, then, sacred, since a sacred place is a place that is filled with power and ability, a place that is important to her, a place that affirms life and her connections with something greater than she is. Whether she sees "the sacred" as her body, the land owned by Sallie Bingham, or Earth as perceived by Carol Snow, depends on where she is in her life.

In *Send My Roots Rain*, Cora learns that she is a woman with rights and responsibilities. The men she traded with did not own her body, and her mother did not own her daughter. She realizes that she is as sacred as the church she is working in only after she starts painting the murals on the church walls as Carole's assistant. As Carole struggled with her lions, she realized that Cora was going through a similar struggle; when the two of them began to paint together, Carole ignored Cora's "loud sighing" because Carole "was determined to let her do her work alone." (141) Carole respected Cora's need for sacred space so that Cora could find the Self that was holy, find it as she paints *her* interpretation of the murals' contents on the walls of the church.

Likewise, Maria Soledad's respect for Cora. After a heated argument over Cora sending/not sending for her daughter, Cora leaves Maria's house defeated and hurt. "and yet . . . Cora was her friend, so she let her go off alone, to think and maybe to gather the courage to act." (47) Cora brings the neglected side of her Self into being only when she has the opportunity to do what she always wanted to do and was good at: paint. When she begins to be the subject of her life in activity, not someone else's object in passivity, she takes action to bring her daughter home, and the healing to wholeness of the self fragmented from the Self begins.

The beginning of Cora's path to healing happens when she realizes that her voice has power, and that she matters. The fight she had with the coyote after he had raped her, and her success at slashing him many times with his own knife is the recalled incident that gives her the remembrance of how personal power could make her strong and worthy and whole. (137)

Dulcie, too, uses a knife to kill a man who steals her power that is her Being. To Dulcie, all Earth is sacred, and men are seen in the same light and on the same level as women, pine needles, meadow flowers, deer, the rock crests, streams, the thicket. Dulcie does not live in a world of hierarchy as Arliss does. Women are valuable to Arliss only for what they can do for him, not for who they are. The same for the desert: what can it do for *him*? When a woman or the desert does for him what he wants, he takes what they give, then he leaves, with no thought of the Other. So, in New York, when Arliss profanes Dulcie by twisting their relationship to suit his ends, Austin shows "that Dulcie, like the land, has a 'natural' right to fight back in order to heal herself."[17]

Carole does not kill a man to regain her power, but she conquers the power animal of the man who held her power. She does so in the vast emptiness of the desert, a place she has feared and found to be "overpowering," even profane; however, the desert eventually becomes a place sacred to Carole as the space where she reunites self to Self. The desert becomes an active agent of Earth, calling nonverbally to Carole in the form of "the dance of the demons." As Carole comes not to fear the desert but respect it, be receptive to what it offers, "dance" with it, the desert works with, not against her.

Maria Milleny needs a physical place to quiet her mind in order to think without interruptions. Catriona's one-room cottage on the west end of the island helps Maria to gain creative images from which to sculpt; it also gives her "sacred time" to come to an understanding of her roots in nature and ancestry.

Both Maria Milleny and Carole come to realize that the growth of natural and ancestral truths requires the germination of the seeds of those truths—personal and artistic—rooting silently and in the dark. If there is no root system established, there are no flowers. Only when the germination has taken root, can the seeds then send up shoots to leaf and flower in the sunlight. The sun and air are needed to flesh out the growing plants/truths, but only after the soil and the rain, in the silences of the underworld darkness, have facilitated the germination and the rooting. The strength and awesome quality of a rose, an apple, or a nasturtium is not in its external beauty, but in the solid core that lies beneath the surface. Honoring the time to germinate is giving that time a sacred quality, a holy quality, a healing quality, a sense of power, and the space one inhabits *in* that time, then, becomes sacred as well.

Two women who cannot find clock time and physical space in order to re-create the whole self are Gertie and her neighbor in the projects, Mrs. Anderson. When she lives in Kentucky, Gertie's house is crowded with a husband and five children, but she always finds space outdoors to feel connected to the universe. Anywhere outdoors: near the stream; in the woods; in the garden digging potatoes; the spot does not matter. Being literally close to the earth make her feel whole, healed, connected to something greater than she. Even the financial poverty her family lives in does not wither her spirit.

With the move to the projects in Detroit, not only is there hardly room to turn around in the cramped quarters they must call home, there is no room outdoors either. There is no room and there is almost no dirt that she could run through her fingers, or step on with her bare feet in order to feel connected to the universe as she did in Kentucky. She does not even have the stars and the moon at night; because the smoke and fumes from the steel mills are so dense, very seldom does she see a star, or the moon. Her soul feels cramped, her spirit is uprooted. There is no medium for her to check her relationship with the natural universe—except the block of cherry wood she shipped from Kentucky. While she works on her block of wood, even in their tiny apartment, she feels "clean." She loses that feeling when she takes the block of wood to the wood lot to be chopped into pieces in order to manufacture objects to sell at the Christmas bazaar in Grosse Pointe.

Like Gertie, Mrs. Anderson felt whole and clean when she and her family were living on their farm in Indiana. In the projects she can find neither time nor space to work on her painting, that which kept her in touch with her Self; in the suburbs, she has the space, but she has no time. Gertie and Mrs. Anderson are two women trying to co-create with the Self. By story's end, Mrs. Anderson has denied the incentive to create even when there are no other pressing needs to attend to; Gertie's responsibility shifts from "whittlin foolishness" to earning money in order to provide food for her family when Clovis chooses to go on strike with his union. Their creative spirits are muzzled by "some many-voiced beast out there, hungry, waiting for them all." (577)

The beast "waiting for them all" was the beast of World War II, because everything during the time period of the novel was geared to feed the god of war. This god had no soul, only a craving emptiness that would never be filled, but that would destroy life at all levels: from Henley giving his bodily life on the battlefield to Gertie and Mrs. Anderson surrendering their creative lives 3,000 miles away from the center of its devouring mouth. Gertie and Mrs. Anderson have no one to help them find time and space in Detroit to enter "the cratered night of female memory" in order to co-create with products from Earth, either blocks of cherry wood or the people in the alley waiting to be painted.

After the war ends, for Gertie the many-voiced beast is the industrial base in Detroit: unions striking; lack of garden space to grow food more cheaply than buying it in a store; acquiring city needs like refrigerators that demand money to purchase, and more money to operate. For Mrs. Anderson, some of the many voices from the beast were from the other suburban women who judged her housekeeping abilities, her children's appearance, her husband's personality, and as a couple, their ability to "fit in" so that her husband can climb the corporate ladder. The singular voice calling to her to paint and to Gertie to carve could not be heard above the din.

Why is there the need for space in the lives of these women? Virginia Woolf wrote in *A Room of One's Own* that a woman who writes or paints or has creative inklings that desire expression needs her own room and time and money to use it in order to create. Alice Walker added to that "and a lock on the door." In *Silences*, Tillie Olsen described what happens to women who have neither their own rooms, nor the money to support themselves, nor the lock on the door: they do not compose. Their silences are not because they were waiting for ideas to germinate; the silences are what Olsen called "unnatural silences" from lacking the room, the money, the time, and the key.

I find it interesting that of the women characters I describe, all of them did understand the need for space and time in order to create their art, craft, or "whittlen foolishness," and recreate the Self. That need, like the need to hear and tell stories, is sometimes more important than food. The space given to act on that need I have defined as "sacred space," because any space that allows me as a woman to be able to hear and respond to the call of Earth's voice and helps me to wholeness is sacred, holy, healing. Since beginning my journey, I have found that nothing is more valuable to me than those opportunities because they lead to personal power and growth, and, eventually, to an understanding of my place in *cosmic* power and growth.

Louise Erdrich writes, "here I am, where I ought to be. A writer must have a place where he or she feels this, a place to love and be irritated with. . . . Knowing a place provides the link between details and meaning. Location, whether it is to abandon it or draw it sharply, is where we start. And place, location in those circumstances, is sacred."[18]

The grandmother narrator in a short story called "Homeland" by Barbara Kingsolver describes the life of one of the fugitive bands of Cherokee who resisted capture and displacement by General Winfield Scott in the 1860s. The grandmother's parents, who had been members of the band, told their daughter how the band survived; the daughter, as an old woman, tells her granddaughter the story. They survived "because they had carried the truth of themselves in a sheltered place inside the flesh, exactly the way a fruit that has gone soft still carries inside itself the clean, hard stone of its future."[19]

After walking the journeys with the women whose stories I chose to read in order to learn more about my own journey, I have come to believe that physical space and uninterrupted time are both vital in order to root self to Self. I also believe that there is another sacred space as important as physical space; it is inner space, psychic space that exists in a special place inside the heart. It is "a sheltered place inside the flesh," surrounded by a darkness and silence so necessary to keep the roots of life vibrant, meaningful, and growing. Without the darkness and silence, the roots do not grow. The food for these roots consists of stories told by trees, humans, stones, rain, thorns, animals, the wind, the desert, seaweed. It is then up to the receiver of the stories to take them "to heart": it is this symbiotic process that roots self to Self by answering Earth's call to healing. It was this process, through my journey, that brought me to wholeness.

In that sacred space, a Self can be born, and die to be born to create again, and again; it is a space where cycles of birth, life, death, and rebirth are respected. It is a space where our powers to create and grow are fertilized. It is a space where we can realize our connectedness with everything living in the universe; it is a space where we can affirm the belief that when harm is done to the rain forests, the rivers, and the deserts, it is done to everything living. It is the place to reweave "the fragments of a shattered universe." It is "homeland." It is the journey into the Self to "discover the secret wishes of the soul." It is in that space where we find truth and recognize, "who am I?"; "where am I from?"; "how did I come to be?"

This inner space, coupled with an exterior place "where I ought to be" and the time to occupy that place, provide the catalyst for the creative act. That creative act can be sculpting, painting, writing, dancing, quilt-making, gardening, or healing a Self that is waiting to be birthed into wholeness. All are creative acts, and *how* we create, which truths we use to form those acts, will determine how we remake and reheal our planet Earth, a most sacred space through which all Earth-creation is born and the fragmented Self is healed.

Notes

Part One
The Stories Begin

1. Irene Zahava, ed., *Hear the Silence: Stories by Women of Myth, Magic and Renewal* (Trumansburg, NY: Crossing Press, 1986), pp. 15–16.

2. Ibid., p. 126.

3. Mircea Eliade, *The Sacred and the Profane* (New York: Harcourt, Brace, 1959), p. 24.

4. Nicole Brossard, "Access to Writing: Ritual of the Written Word," in *Trivia: A Journal of Ideas* 8 (Winter 1986): 8–14.

5. Carol Christ, "Why Women Need the Goddess: Phenomenological, Psychological, and Political Reflections, in Carol Christ and Judith Plaskow, eds., *Womanspirit Rising: A Feminist Reader in Religion* (New York: Harper & Row, 1979), p. 277.

6. See "The Goddess as Muse" by Toni Flores in Ivan Brady, ed., *Anthropological Poetics* (Maryland: Rowman & Littlefield, 1991), pp. 137–153.

7. In personal correspondence with Lorraine Anderson, I have learned that some European women have requested that she do for them what she did for the women of the United States. What is happening in women's prose and poetry about nature today, then, is what happened to the goddess movement when, in 1976, Merlin Stone published *When God*

Was a Woman; it is on the threshold of bursting a dike and allowing the dammed-up waters of women's true relationship to nature to flow freely again. This is in opposition to the lie that men identify with culture and women with nature, and, in that identification is the hierarchy that culture is superior and nature is inferior. Since finding Lorraine via her book, I have enjoyed an on-going correspondence with her these years; she introduced me to Mary Austin's *Cactus Thorn* and to Sally Bingham's work.

8. Elizabeth A. Flynn, "Gender and Reading," in Elizabeth A. Flynn and Patrocinio P. Schweickart, eds., *Gender and Reading: Essays on Readers, Texts, and Contexts* (Baltimore: Johns Hopkins, 1986), p. 268. What follows is my interpretation of Prof. Flynn's description of reader-response criticism.

9. Ibid., p. 48.

10. Elizabeth Minnich, *Transforming Knowledge* (Philadelphia: Temple University Press, 1990), pp. 37–38.

Part Two
Storytelling and Truthtelling: "I remember and I recall."

1. Merlin Stone, *When God Was a Woman* (New York: Dial Press, 1976), pp. 62–69.

2. Ibid., p. 66.

3. Mary Condron, *The Serpent and the Goddess: Women, Religion and Power in Celtic Ireland* (San Francisco: Harper, 1989), p. xxiii.

4. Gerda Lerner, *The Creation of Patriarchy* (New York: Oxford, 1986), p. 6.

5. Stone, p. 1.

6. Christ, p. 277.

7. This is from a presentation that Anne Cameron gave in Oswego, New York in the spring of 1987.

8. The Telling It Book Collective, eds., *Telling It: Women and Language Across Cultures* (Vancouver: Press Gang Publishers, 1990), pp. 16–17.

9. As Paula Gunn Allen claims, and as some of her foremothers remember, historically Native women are honored because they mimic the creative power of Mother Earth. Thus many Native women and men have not been reared in a system where women are punished for being the ancestors of their foremother, Eve, who brought evil and pain into the world. Eve is not their foremother. (Personal conversation with Jeanne Shenandoah, eldest daughter of Audrey Shenandoah, Onondaga, and Dr. Sally Roesch Wagner.)

10. Paula Gunn Allen, *Spider Woman's Granddaughters* (Boston: Beacon, 1986), p. 20.

11. Sun Bear, Wabun, and Barry Weinstock, *The Path of Power* (New York: Prentice Hall, 1987), p. 94.

12. Louise Erdrich, "Where I Ought to Be: A Writer's Sense of Place." *New York Times Book Review*, 28 July 1985, p. 23.

13. Joseph Bruchac, ed. *Survival This Way: Interviews With American Indian Poets* (Tucson: University of Arizona Press, 1987), pp. xi–xiii.

14. Christ, p. 277.

15. Jane Yolen made this point in her keynote speech at a children's literature conference called "Fall Institute on Fantasy" that I attended in Rochester, NY on September 21, 1991.

16. Marilyn Sanders Mobley, *Folk Roots and Mythic Wings in Sara Orne Jewett and Toni Morrison: The Cultural Function of Narrative* (Baton Rouge: Louisiana State University Press, 1991), pp. 175–176.

17. Gabriele Lusser Rico, *Writing the Natural Way* (Los Angeles: Jeremy Tarcher, 1983). Professor Rico gives credit to psychologist Renée Fuller for this concept, as well as inventing the word "storying."

18. See Stone, *When God Was a Woman*, Lerner, *The Creation of Patriarchy* and Elinor Gaden, *The Once and Future Goddess* (San Francisco: Harper, 1989).

19. Leslie Marmon Silko, *Storyteller* (New York: Seaver, 1981), dedication page.

20. David Leeming, *The World of Myth* (New York: Oxford University Press, 1990), p. 8.

21. Barry Lopez, *Crow and Weasel* (San Francisco: North Point, 1990), p. 48.

22. Ibid, p. 48.

23. Lynne Rosenthal, "The Development of Consciousness in Lucy Boston's *The Children of Green Knowe*," from *The Annual of The Modern Language Association Group on Children's Literature* (New Haven: Yale University Press, 1980), p. 59.

24. Lucy Boston, *The Children of Green Knowe* (New York: Harcourt, 1954, 1955), p. 60.

25. Alice Walker, *In Search of Our Mothers' Gardens* (New York: Harcourt Brace, 1983).

26. Toni Morrison, "Rootedness: The Ancestor as Foundation," in Mari Evans, ed. *Black Women Writers (1950–1980): A Critical Evaluation* (New York: Doubleday, 1984), p. 344.

27. Rozsika Parker, *The Subversive Stitch: Embroidery and the Making of the Feminine* (Great Britain: the Women's Press, 1984), preface.

28. Ibid., p. 11.

29. Ibid., p. 198.

30. Ibid., p. 201.

31. Judy Chicago, *The Dinner Party* (New York: Anchor, 1979), p. 15.

32. Nellie Morton, *The Journey is Home* (Boston: Beacon Press, 1985), pp. xiv–xv.

33. Beth Brant, *Mohawk Trail* (Ithaca: Firebrand Press, 1985), pp. 20–21.

34. Paula Gunn Allen, *The Sacred Hoop: Rediscovering the Feminine in American Indian Tradition* (Boston: Beacon Press, 1986), p. 243.

35. Susan Glaspell, "A Jury of Her Peers" in Edward J. O'Brien, ed. *The Best Short Stories of 1918* (Boston: Small, Maynard, 1918), pp. 271–73.

36. Annette Kolodny, *The Land Before Her: Fantasy and Experience of the American Frontiers, 1630–1860* (Chapel Hill: University of North Carolina Press, 1984), p. 120.

37. Ibid., p. 121.

38. Ibid., p. 54. Kolodny makes it clear in her preface that she is writing of white, middle-class women from the eastern United States who could write the diaries, journals, letters, and novels that she found. Lost are the thoughts and experiences of the ones who could not write. Lost to research, that is. Not lost to the imagination and ancestral memory of writers like Toni Morrison, who heard her ancestors' oral stories. See Morrison's speech, "The Site of Memory" in *Inventing the Truth*, edited by William Zinsser, pp. 101–120.

39. There was an insert printed in the Syracuse *Post Standard*, June 15, 1994, p. A–8 called "Declining Numbers," from *Zero Population Growth*, Washington, D.C. The contents of the insert reveal that women own 1% of the world's property while they earn 10% of the world's income and perform 66% of the world's work. Gardening takes up only a little space, farming a lot of space. It is no wonder that women, then, are "gardeners, not farmers."

40. Ben Logan, *The Land Remembers* (Minocqua: Heartland, 1985), p. 5.

41. Ibid., p. 275.

42. Ibid., pp. 276–77.

43. Aurora Levins Morales and Rosario Morales, *Getting Home Alive* (Ithaca: Firebrand Press, 1986), pp. 132–94.

44. Patricia MacLaughlin, *Sarah, Plain and Tall* (New York: Harper, 1985), p. 41.

45. Walker, pp. 241–43.

46. Carol Snow, "The Winter Dreams of Bears," in Joseph Bruchac, ed. *New Voices From the Longhouse* (Greenfield Center: Greenfield Review Press, 1989), pp. 238–39.

47. Ibid.

48. Ibid.

49. Lorraine Anderson, ed., *Sister of the Earth: Women's Prose and Poetry About Nature* (New York: Viking, 1991), pp. xvii–xviii.

50. Bruchac, *New Voices From the Longhouse*, p. 271.

51. Allen, *The Sacred Hoop*, pp. 41–45.

52. Ibid., pp. 7, 32, 252–55, 260–61.

53. For a recent experience of how the Mothers of the Longhouse are being called upon to settle a serious conflict taking place in the Onondaga Nation, see the story of the dispute between the Onondagas who own businesses and collect and keep the cigarette tax and the chiefs who say that part of that revenue belongs to the whole Nation. "Mothers of the Nation," Syracuse *Herald American*, June 26, 1994, Sec. E, p. 7 is one article articulating the conflict. The conflict began in 1988.

54. Marilou Awiakta, "Amazons in Appalachia," in Beth Brant, ed., *A Gathering of Spirit: Writing and Art by North American Indian Women* (Maine: Sinister Wisdom, 1984), p. 125.

55. Walker, p. 276.

56. Quoted in an interview reprinted in the Syracuse *Post Standard*, July 22, 1992.

57. Barry Lopez, *Crossing Open Ground* (New York: Charles Scribner's Sons, 1988), pp. 65–67. I assume that Lopez thinks that women feel

the same sense, although throughout the book he uses "he." His use of "he" became distracting for me, considering the book was published in 1988 and he is speaking of eternal and universal theories. In spite of his lack of gender consciousness, his writing evoked many thoughts in me on truth and narrative that are similar to my own.

58. Valerie Andrews, *A Passion For This Earth* (San Francisco: Harper, 1990), p. 4.

59. Toni Morrison, "The Site of Memory," in Zinsser, ed., p. 119.

60. Logan, preface, np.

61. Lopez, *Crossing Open Ground*, p. 69.

62. Ibid., p. 69.

63. Bobette Perrone, Henriette Stockel and Victoria Krueger, *Medicine Women, Curanderas and Women Doctors* (Norman: University of Oklahoma Press, 1989), pp. 36–38.

64. Mary Austin, *The Land of Little Rain*, 1903 (New York: Penguin, 1988), p. 78. For details of Mary Austin's definition of and conflict with civilization, read her autobiography, *Earth Horizon*.

65. Terry Tempest Williams, *Refuge: An Unnatural History of Family and Place* (New York: Pantheon, 1991), pp. 281–90.

66. Carol Bruchac, Linda Hogan and Judith McDaniel, eds., *The Stories We Hold Secret: Tales of Women's Spiritual Development* (Greenfield Center: Greenfield Review Press, 1986), pp. x–xiv.

67. Sally Carrighar, *Home to the Wilderness* (Boston: Houghton Mifflin, 1973), pp. vii–viii.

68. Ibid., pp. 194–95.

69. Ibid., p. 194.

70. Tillie Olsen, *Silences*, 1963 (New York: Delacorte Press, 1978), p. 253.

71. Jeanne Achterberg, *Woman as Healer* (Boston: Shambala Publications, 1990), p. 103.

72. For a thorough understanding of the witch hunts, read Barbara Walker, *The Crone* (San Francisco: Harper, 1985); to realize how truly fragmented our Western society is when it comes to labeling specific conceptual errors in thinking as true knowledge, read Elizabeth Minnich, *Transforming Knowledge*; for an eye-opening and at times shocking history of family violence in modern Europe and United States, read Alice Miller, *For Your Own Good: Hidden Cruelty in Child-Rearing and the Roots of Violence*. Trans. Hildegarde and Hunter Hannum (New York: Farrar, Strauss, and Giroux, Inc., 1983); for the history of atomic bombing in the American West, read Terry Tempest Williams, *Refuge*.

73. Harvey Arden and Steve Wall, *Wisdomkeepers: Meetings with Native American Spiritual Elders* (Oregon: Beyond Words, 1990), pp. 26–27.

74. Rachel Carson, *The Sea Around Us*, 1950 (Oxford: Oxford University Press, 1989), pp. 13–14.

75. Allen, *The Sacred Hoop*, p. 11.

76. Clarissa Pinkola Estes, *Women Who Run With the Wolves* (New York: Ballantine, 1992), p. 9.

Part Three
"Tell me a story that's true."

1. Carol Christ, *Diving Deep and Surfacing: Women Writers on Spiritual Quest* (Boston: Beacon, 1980), p. 5.

2. Mary Austin, *Earth Horizon* (Boston: Houghton Mifflin, 1932), p. 33.

3. Melody Graulich, "Afterward" in Mary Austin, *Cactus Thorn* (Reno: University of Nevada Press, 1988), pp. 110–18.

4. Shirley Neuman and Smaro Kamboureli, eds., *A Mazing Space: Writing Canadian Women Writing* (Alberta: Longspoon, 1986), p. 276.

5. Graulich, p. 116.

6. Minnich, p. 186.

7. Mary Austin, *Cactus Thorn* (Reno: University of Nevada Press, 1988), p. 3. Subsequent references to this novel are given parenthetically in the text.

8. Sandra Ingerman, *Soul Retrieval: Mending the Fragmented Self* (San Francisco: Harper, 1991), p. 108.

9. For a detailed explanation of disorder, realignment, and the cosmos, see Paula Gunn Allen's *Grandmothers of the Light*, 6–9, 15–20. See also "Myth, Magic, and Medicine in the Modern World" in the same text, 165–170.

10. Minnich, p. 186.

11. Harriette Arnow, *The Dollmaker*, 1954 (New York: Avon Books, 1972), p. 91. Subsequent references to this novel are given parenthetically in the text.

12. Tillie Olsen, *Silences*, 1963 (New York: Delacorte Press, 1978), p. 34.

13. Ibid., p. 35.

14. Ibid.

15. Ibid., p. 43.

16. Eliade, p. 24.

17. William Eckley, *Harriette Arnow* (New York: Twayne Publishers, 1974), p. 42.

18. Olsen, p. 219.

19. Walker, p. 238.

20. Virginia Woolf, *The Death of the Moth and Other Essays* (New York: Harcourt, Brace and Co., 1942), p. 236.

21. Olsen, pp. 33–34.

22. Ibid., p. 39.

23. Adrienne Rich, *Poems: Selected and New, 1950–1974* (New York: Norton, 1975), p. 228.

24. Sandra Gilbert and Susan Gubar, *The Madwoman in the Attic: The Woman Writer and the Nineteenth–Century Literary Imagination* (New Haven: Yale University Press, 1979), p. 99.

25. For a list of living artists (and photos of their works,) who have used artistic media to celebrate their discoveries when they made this journey, read Elinor Gaden, *The Once and Future Goddess*.

26. Ellen Galford, *The Fires of Bride* (Ithaca, NY: Firebrand Books, 1988), pp. 9–10. Subsequent references to this novel are given parenthetically in the text.

27. In "Demise of Brigit" in *The Serpent and the Goddess*, Mary Condron spares no description, no matter how harsh, on how the church fathers, in a twelfth-century reform movement, changed Brigit's role from mother goddess to virgin saint, thus changing the image and reality of Brigit and all she symbolized to Celtic and Gaelic women and men up until that time.

28. For a fascinating and historical account of the transfer of power from the outer-lying nunneries in Ireland, Scotland and Wales, read Part II "The Age of Brigit" in Mary Condron's book *The Serpent and the Goddess*.

29. In a publication called *Stitched from the Soul: Slave Quilts from the Ante-Bellum South*, Gladys-Marie Fry uncovered that the reason so many women slaves made quilts in the nineteenth-century South was because they were denied the freedom to read and write. So they stitched their stories into the quilts. Their African ancestors had used their ability to stitch and create freely. The slaves reached back into ancestral memory for that heritage and applied it to making certain their stories got recorded through the quilts. Like Beth Brant's aunts, most of those quilts were done in secret and unfortunately have been lost, but some of them were not. See p. 83 of her text for more on this phenomenon.

30. For a detailed explanation of the properties from the sea that our blood carries, see Rachel Carson's, *The Sea Around Us*.

31. These rituals and charms and the processes by which one uses them can be found in *Jambalaya* (San Francisco: Harper, 1985) by Luisah Teish. Teish is a priestess of Oshun, the Yoruba (West Africa) goddess of

love and art, and a ritualist of the Seven African Powers. Her explanations of these Powers and rituals overlap with the rituals and objects that Ellen Galford sketches into the character and beliefs of Catriona.

32. Christ, *Diving Deep and Surfacing*, p. xiv.

33. Merlin Stone, *Ancient Mirrors of Modern Womanhood* (Boston: Beacon, 1991), pp. 65–66.

34. Farrar, Janet and Stewart Farrar, *The Witches' Goddess* (Custer, WA: Phoenix Press, 1987), p. 96.

35. I have culled these details from Condron's *The Serpent and the Goddess*, the Farrars' *The Witches' Goddess*, Stone's *Ancient Mirrors of Womanhood* and Galford's *The Fires of Bride*.

36. In October 1992, 500 people from 41 countries gathered in Crete to participate in workshops at a conference called "First International Minoan Celebration of Friendship." The participants "learned what archaeologists and anthropologists have confirmed, that human beings lived in cooperative partnerships for thousands of years before the dominator model took over" (from *The Owl Observer: National Newspaper of the Older Women's League*, Jan/Feb. 1993, p. 4.)

37. Gilbert and Gubar, p. 76.

38. Virginia Woolf, *A Room of One's Own*, 1929 (New York: Harcourt, Brace, 1957), p. 86.

39. I drew this name from the title of E. M. Broner's novel *A Weave of Women*, (Bloomington: Indiana University Press, 1985). When I read Broner's novel, and then read Gómez-Vega's, I saw a perfect fit in the context of a community of women.

40. Ibis Gómez-Vega, *Send My Roots Rain* (San Francisco: Aunt Lute, 1991), p. 18. Subsequent references to this novel are given parenthetically in the text.

41. Sonia Saldivar-Hull, "Feminism on the Border: From Gender Politics to Geopolitics," in Florence Howe, ed., *Tradition and the Talents of Women* (Urbana: Univ. of Illinois Press, 1991), pp. 297–98.

42. Ibid., p. 298.

43. Christ, *Diving Deep and Surfacing*, p. 17.

44. Buffie Johnson, *Lady of the Beasts: Ancient Images of the Goddess and Her Sacred Animals* (San Francisco: Harper, 1988), p. 122.

45. Walker, p. 252.

46. Allen, *The Sacred Hoop*, p. 247.

47. Lucille Daniel, "Standing Our Ground: Conversations with Terry Tempest Williams," *Sojourner: The Women's Forum*, Feb. 1993, p. 19.

48. Christ, *Diving Deep and Surfacing*, pp. xiv, 53.

Part Four
Sacred Spaces: the need to name and claim them in our lives

1. Elizabeth Dodson Gray, *Sacred Dimensions of Women's Experience* (Wellesley: Round Table, 1988), p. 1.

2. Ibid., p. 2.

3. Condron, p. xvii.

4. Gray, p. 2.

5. Ibid.

6. Ibid. Whether Gray meant *all* women and *all* men, I don't know. She does not make distinctions between the genders or races.

7. Ibid.

8. Walker, p. 43.

9. Gray, p. 4.

10. Ibid., pp. 4–5. Updating Gray's insight of 1988 that women's bodies are still considered profane and unclean, I refer you to issue eighteen of *woman of power*, fall 1990, called "Women's Bodies" and *Possessing the Secret of Joy* by Alice Walker (New York: Harcourt, 1992). Also, note our culture's attitude toward menstruation. There are all kinds of products to hide the act and time and odor of menses. In pre-patriarchal cul-

tures, however, menses were held to be a sacred, visioning, inwardly powerful time; the women would gather something from Earth such as moss and bleed into it. The act of bleeding into an element from Earth indicated that the women saw their "moon time" as a time to return something from their bodies back to their life-giver, Earth. Collected menses were then used as a fertilizer. That point of view has been transformed from a life-enhancing act to a death-enhancing act when football fans shout during a game, "Blood makes the grass grow!"

11. Teish, p. 76.

12. Evans, ed., p. 344.

13. Allen, *The Sacred Hoop*, pp. 72–73.

14. *Telling It*, pp. 14–29.

15. Margaret Atwood, *Surfacing*, 1972 (New York: Random House, 1990), p. 170.

16. Eliade, p. 63.

17. Graulich, p. 112.

18. Erdrich, pp. 22–23.

19. Barbara Kingsolver, *Homeland and Other Stories* (New York: Harper, 1989), p. 2.

Works Cited

Achterberg, Jeanne. *Woman as Healer*. Boston: Shambala, 1990.

Allen, Paula Gunn. *The Sacred Hoop: Rediscovering the Feminine in American Indian Tradition*. Boston: Beacon, 1986.

———. *Spider Woman's Granddaughters*. Boston: Beacon, 1989.

Anderson, Lorraine. *Sisters of the Earth: Women's Prose and Poetry About Nature*. New York: Viking, 1991.

Andrews, Valerie. *A Passion for this Earth*. San Francisco: Harper, 1990.

Arden, Harvey and Steve Wall. *Wisdomkeepers: Meetings with Native American Spiritual Elders*. Oregon: Beyond Words, 1990.

Arnow, Harriette. *The Dollmaker*. 1954. New York: Avon, 1972.

Atwood, Margaret. *Surfacing*. 1972. New York: Random House, 1990.

Austin, Mary. *Cactus Thorn*. Reno: University of Nevada Press, 1988.

———. *Earth Horizon*. Boston: Houghton Mifflin, 1932.

———. *The Land of Little Rain*. 1903. New York: Penguin, 1988.

Bingham, Sallie. "A Woman's Land." *The Amicus Journal* Fall 1990: 36–38.

Boston, Lucy. *The Children of Green Knowe*. New York: Harcourt, 1954, 1955.

Brady, Ivan, ed. *Anthropological Poetics*. MD: Rowman & Littlefield, 1991.

Brant, Beth, ed. *A Gathering of Spirit: Writing and Art by North American Indian Women*. Maine: Sinister Wisdom, 1984.

———. *Mohawk Trail*. Ithaca: Firebrand, 1985.

Broner, E. M. *A Weave of Women*. Bloomington: Indiana University Press, 1985.

Brossard, Nicole. "Access to Writing: Ritual of the Written Word." *Trivia: A Journal of Ideas* 8 Winter 1986: 8–14.

Brother Eagle, Sister Sky. "A message from Chief Seattle." illustrated by Susan Jeffers. New York: Dial, 1991.

Bruchac, Carol, Linda Hogan and Judith McDaniel, eds. *The Stories We Hold Secret: Tales of Women's Spiritual Development*. Greenfield Center: Greenfield Review Press, 1986.

Bruchac, Joseph, ed. *New Voices From the Longhouse*. Greenfield Center: Greenfield Review Press, 1989.

———. *Survival This Way: Interviews with American Indian Poets*. Tucson: University of Arizona Press, 1987.

Burnett, Frances Hodgson. *The Secret Garden*. Philadelphia: J. B. Lippincott, 1911.

Burns, M.C. "Mothers of the Nation," *Herald American* [Syracuse, NY], June 26, 1994, Sec. E, p. 7.

Carrighar, Sally. *Home to the Wilderness*. Boston: Houghton Mifflin, 1973.

Carson, Rachel. *The Sea Around Us*. 1950. Oxford: Oxford University Press, 1989.

———. *Silent Spring*. Boston: Houghton Mifflin, 1962.

Chicago, Judy. *The Dinner Party*. New York: Anchor, 1979.

Christ, Carol. *Diving Deep and Surfacing: Women Writers on Spiritual Quest*. Boston: Beacon, 1980.

Christ, Carol P. and Judith Plaskow, eds. *Womanspirit Rising: A Feminist Reader in Religion*. New York: Harper, 1979.

Condron, Mary. *The Serpent and the Goddess: Women, Religion and Power in Celtic Ireland.* San Francisco: Harper, 1989.

Daniel, Lucille. "Standing Our Ground: Conversations with Terry Tempest Williams." *Sojourner: The Women's Forum* Feb. 1993:1+.

Eckley, William. *Harriette Arnow.* New York: Twayne, 1974.

Eisler, Riane. *The Chalice and the Blade.* San Francisco: Harper,1987.

Eliade, Mircea. *The Sacred and the Profane.* New York: Harcourt, 1959.

Erdrich, Louise. "Where I Ought to Be: A Writer's Sense of Place." *New York Times Book Review* 28 July 1985, 1+.

Estes, Clarissa Pinkola. *Women Who Run with the Wolves: Myths and Stories of the Wild Woman Archetype.* New York: Ballentine,1992.

Evans, Marie, ed. *Black Women Writers (1950–1980).* Garden City, New York: Doubleday, 1984.

Farrar, Janet and Stewart Farrar. *The Witches' Goddess.* Custer, WA: Phoenix, 1987.

Flynn, Elizabeth A. and Patrocinio P. Schweickart, eds. *Gender and Reading: Essays on Readers, Texts, and Contexts.* Baltimore: Johns Hopkins,1986.

Fry, Gladys-Marie. *Stitched From the Soul: Slave Quilts from the Ante-Bellum South.* New York: Dutton, 1990.

Gadon, Elinor W. *The Once and Future Goddess: A Sweeping Visual Chronicle of the Sacred Female and Her Reemergence in the Cultural Mythology of our Time.* San Francisco: Harper, 1989.

Galford, Ellen. *The Fires of Bride.* Ithaca: Firebrand, 1988.

Gilbert, Sandra and Susan Gubar. *The Madwoman in the Attic: The Woman Writer and the Nineteenth–Century Literary Imagination.* New Haven: Yale University Press, 1979.

Glaspell, Susan. "A Jury of Her Peers." *The Best Short Stories of 1918.* Ed. Edward J. O'Brien. Boston: Small, Maynard, 1918. 256–82.

Gómez-Vega, Ibis. *Send My Roots Rain.* San Francisco: Aunt Lute,1991.

Graulich, Melody. Afterword. *Cactus Thorn*. By Mary Austin. Reno: University of Nevada Press, 1988. 101–122.

Gray, Elizabeth Dodson, ed. *Sacred Dimensions of Women's Experience*. Wellesley: Round Table, 1988.

Ingerman, Sandra. *Soul Retrieval: Mending the Fragmented Self*. San Francisco: Harper, 1991.

"Interview with Alice Walker." *Post Standard* [Syracuse, NY] 22 July, 1992.

Johnson, Buffie. *Lady of the Beasts: Ancient Images of the Goddess and Her Sacred Animals*. San Francisco: Harper, 1988.

Kingsolver, Barbara. *Homeland and Other Stories*. New York: Harper, 1989.

Kolodny, Annette. *The Land Before Her: Fantasy and Experience of the American Frontiers, 1630–1860*. Chapel Hill: University of North Carolina Press, 1984.

Leeming, David Adams. *The World of Myth*. New York: Oxford University Press, 1990.

Lerner, Gerda. *The Creation of Patriarchy*. New York: Oxford, 1986.

Logan, Ben. *The Land Remembers*. 1975. Minocqua: Heartland, 1985.

Lopez, Barry. *Crossing Open Ground*. Scribner's, 1988.

———. *Crow and Weasel*. San Francisco: North Point, 1990.

MacLaughlin, Patricia. *Sarah, Plain and Tall*. New York: Harper, 1985.

Miller, Alice. *For Your Own Good: Hidden Cruelty in Child-Rearing and the Roots of Violence*. Trans. Hildegarde and Hunter Hannum. New York: Farrar, 1983.

Minnich, Elizabeth. *Transforming Knowledge*. Philadelphia: Temple University Press, 1990.

Mobley, Marilyn Sanders. *Folk Roots and Mythic Wings in Sara Orne Jewett and Toni Morrison: The Cultural Function of Narrative*. Baton Rouge: Louisiana State University Press, 1991.

Morales, Aurora Levins and Rosario. *Getting Home Alive*. Ithaca: Firebrand, 1986.

Morrison, Toni. "Rootedness: The Ancestor as Foundation." In *Black Women Writers (1950–1980): A Critical Evaluation*, edited by Marie Evans. New York: Doubleday, 1984.

————. "The Site of Memory." In *Inventing the Truth*, edited by William Zinsser. Boston: Houghton Mifflin, 1987.

Morton, Nelle. *The Journey is Home*. Boston: Beacon, 1985.

Neuman, Shirley and Smaro Kamboureli, eds. *A Mazing Space: Writing Canadian Women Writing*. Alberta: Longspoon, 1986.

Olsen, Tillie. *Silences*. 1963. New York: Delacorte Press, 1978.

"OWLS Study Partnership in Crete." *OWL Observer* Jan/Feb. 1993: 4.

Parker, Rozsika. *The Subversive Stitch: Embroidery and the Making of the Feminine*. Great Britain: The Women's Press, 1984.

Perrone, Bobette, Henrietta Stockel and Victoria Krueger. *Medicine Women, Curanderas and Women Doctors*. Norman: University of Oklahoma Press, 1989.

Rich, Adrienne. *Poems: Selected and New, 1950–1974*. New York: Norton, 1975.

Rico, Gabriele Lusser. *Writing the Natural Way*. Los Angeles: Tarcher, 1983.

Rosenthal, Lynne. "The Development of Consciousness in Lucy Boston's *The Children of Green Knowe*," from *The Annual of The Modern Language Association Group on Children's Literature*. New Haven: Yale University Press, 1980. 55–67.

Saldivar-Hull, Sonia. "Feminism on the Border: From Gender Politics to Geopolitics." *Tradition and the Talents of Women*. Ed. Florence Howe. Urbana: University of Illinois Press, 1991. 292–307.

Shenandoah, Jeanne. "Native Ways." SUNY/Oswego, 18 Nov. 1992.

Silko, Leslie Marmon. *Storyteller*. New York: Seaver, 1981.

Stone, Merlin. *Ancient Mirrors of Womanhood*. Boston: Beacon, 1991.

————. *When God Was a Woman*. New York: Dial, 1976.

Sun Bear, Wabun, and Barry Weinstock. *The Path of Power*. New York: Prentice Hall, 1987.

Teish, Luisah. *Jambalaya: The Natural Woman's Book of Personal Charms and Practical Rituals*. San Francisco: Harper, 1985.

The Telling It Book Collective, eds. *Telling It: Women and Language Across Cultures*. Vancouver: Press Gang, 1990.

Wagner, Sally Roesch. "The Iroquois Influence on the 19th Century U. S. Women's Rights Movement: A Dialogue." SUNY/Oswego, 18 Nov. 1992.

Walker, Alice. *In Search of Our Mothers' Gardens: Womanist Prose*. New York: Harcourt, 1983.

————. *Possessing the Secret of Joy*. New York: Harcourt, 1992.

Walker, Barbara. *The Crone: Woman of Age, Wisdom and Power*. San Francisco: Harper, 1985.

Williams, Terry Tempest. *Pieces of White Shell*. 1984. Albuquerque: University of New Mexico Press, 1987.

————. *Refuge, An Unnatural History of Family and Place*. New York: Pantheon, 1991.

woman of power, fall, 1990: issue eighteen.

Woolf, Virginia. *A Room of One's Own*. 1929. New York: Harcourt, 1957.

————. *The Death of the Moth and Other Essays*. New York: Harcourt, Brace and Company, 1942.

Yolen, Jane. "Heroes in Fantasy." *Fall Institute on Fantasy*. Rochester: 21 September 1991.

Zahava, Irene, ed. *Hear the Silence: Stories by Women of Myth, Magic and Renewal*. Trumansburg: The Crossing Press, 1986.

Zinsser, William, ed. *Inventing the Truth*. Boston: Houghton Mifflin, 1987.

Index

Achterberg, Jeanne, 52
"After the Invasion," 40–41
Allen, Paula Gunn, x, 10, 19, 22,
   29–30, 40–41, 52, 54, 155, 174
"Amazons in Appalachia," 42
Amicus Journal, The, 33
Anderson, Lorraine, xiv, 13–14, 40
Andrews, Valerie, 43–44
Armstrong, Jeanette, 19, 174
Arnow, Harriette, 7, 57, 60, 61, 89–115
Atwood, Margaret, 158
Austin, Mary, 7, 47, 57, 60, 65–88, 99
Awiakta, Marilou, 41–42

Bingham, Sallie, 33–34, 175
Blatchford, Herb, 47
Boston, Lucy, 24–25, 45
Bowles, Jane, 111
Boynton, Linda, xi
Brant, Beth, 28–29, 40, 41
Brossard, Nicole, 9, 10, 58
Bruchac, Joseph, 21
Budapest, Z, 10
Burnett, Frances Hodgson, 36

Cactus Thorn, 7, 57, 59, 65–88
Cameron, Anne, 5, 10, 19
Carrighar, Sally, 50–52, 55, 58, 94
Carson, Rachel, 13, 17

Cather, Willa, 13
Chalice and the Blade, The, 11
Chicago, Judy, 28
Children of Green Knowe, The, 24
Christ, Carol, 10, 19, 57, 152, 158, 161,
   168
Collins, Sheila, 18
Condron, Mary, 10, 18
Creation of Patriarchy, The, 18
Crossing Open Ground, 43
Crossings, 66
Crow and Weasel, 23, 46

Deloria, Vine, 21
Dillard, Annie, 13
Dinner Party, The, 28
Dollmaker, The, 7, 57, 58, 89–115, 151

Earth Horizon, 65
Ecotone, x
Eisler, Riane, 10, 11
Eliade, Mircea, 8, 175
Erdrich, Louise, 20, 180

Fires of Bride, The, 7, 57, 58, 117–141,
   143
Flynn, Elizabeth A., 14–15, 22, 80
Fuller, Margaret Crane, 33
Fuller, Renée, 22

Gaden, Elinor, 10
Galford, Ellen, 7, 57, 61–62, 117–41
"Gender and Reading," 14
Getting Home Alive, 35–36
Gimbutas, Marija, 10
Glaspell, Susan, 31, 99
Gómez-Vega, Ibis, xv, 7, 57, 62, 143–69
Graulich, Melody, 65, 80
Gray, Elizabeth Dodson, 171–73
Green, Maxine, xi

Harjo, Joy, 40, 41
Hitler, Adolf, 53
Hobson, Gary, 21
Hogan, Linda, 40, 41, 49–50
"Homeland," 180
Home to the Wilderness, 50–52
Hopkins, Gerard Manley, 143
Hurston, Zora Neale, 25

Ingerman, Sandra, 85
Isaacs, Dr. Susanna, 51

Jambalaya, 174
Jeffers, Susan, 174
Johnson, Buffie, 10
"Jury of Her Peers, A," 31–32

Kahn, Annie, 46
Kingsolver, Barbara, 180
Kolodny, Annette, 32–33, 34
Krall, Florence, x

Lambert, Betty, 66
"Land and Narrative," 43
Land Before Her, The, 32
Land Remembers, The, 34, 44–45
Leeming, David, 23
Leopold, Aldo, 13, 34
Lerner, Gerda, 18
Logan, Ben, 34–35, 44
Lopez, Barry, 23, 43–46, 52, 54, 55

MacLaughlin, Patricia, 37
"Magic in a World of Magic," 5, 60
Minnich, Elizabeth, xiii, 15–16, 66–67, 71
Mobley, Marilyn Sanders, 21–22
Mohawk Trail, 29
Morales, Aurora Levins, 35–36
Morales, Rosario, 35
Morrison, Toni, 25–26, 44, 174
Morton, Nelle, 28
Muir, John. 13

O'Keeffe, Georgia, 28, 67
Olsen, Tillie, xiv, 52, 60, 98–99, 110, 115, 153, 179

Parker, Rozsika, 27–28, 131
Pieces of White Shell, 47–48
Plath, Sylvia, 99

Refuge, x, 48–49
Renz, Dr. Carl, 51
Rich, Adrienne, 117
Rico, Gabriele Lusser, 22
Room of One's Own, A, 179
Rose, Wendy, 21

Sacred Dimensions of Women's Experiences, 170–73
Sanchez, Carol Lee, 10, 19, 54
Sarah, Plain and Tall, 37
Schweickart, Patrocinio P., 15
Scott, General Winfield, 180
Sears, Vickie L., 5–6
Seattle, Chief, 174
Send My Roots Rain, 7, 57, 59, 143–169, 175
Serpent and the Goddess, The, 18
"Sex, Class and Race Intersections/Visions of Women of Color," 54
Shenandoah, Audrey, 54
Silences, 179

Silent Spring, 17
Silko, Leslie Marmon, x, 19, 22, 40, 41
Sisters of the Earth, 13–14, 40
Smedley, Agnes, 99
Snow, Carol, 38–40, 44, 52, 175
Spencer, Joan, xiii, 167
Spider Woman's Granddaughters, x, 20
Steffens, Lincoln, 66
"Sticktalk," 5–6
Stone, Merlin, 10, 17, 18
Stories We Hold Secret, The, 49–50
Storyteller, x, 22
Subversive Stitch, The, 131
Sun Bear, 20
Surfacing, 158, 175
Survival This Way, 21

Teish, Luisah, xiv, 10, 174
Thoreau, Henry David, 13
Tremblay, Gail, 40–41

Walker, Alice, 10, 25, 37, 42, 48, 113, 155, 173, 174, 179
When God Was a Woman, 19
"Where I Ought to Be: A Writer's Sense of Place," 20–21, 180
"Why Women Need the Goddess," 10
Williams, Terry Tempest, x, 47–49
"Winter Dreams of Bears, The," 38–40
Wittig, Monica, 19
"A Woman's Land," 33
Woolf, Virginia, 115, 140, 144, 168, 179

Yolen, Jane, 21